WISCONSIN SAMPLER

Edited by Sue E. McCoy
Illustrated by Kathleen A. Brown

Northword

P.O. Box 5634 • Madison, Wisconsin 53705

Designed by Gryphon Studio.

Typeset by Jane Rundell Typography.

Printed in the United States of America by George Banta Co., Inc.

First Printing 1983.

"Guides of Yesteryear" and "Pearl Diver" by Mel Ellis, and "Paul Bunyan's Cookbook, Parts I-IV" by Alonzo W. Pond all reprinted by permission of the Larry Sternig Literary Agency. "A Bout with Dame Fashion," by Fred L. Holmes, reprinted from *Side Roads: Excursions Into Wisconsin's Past* by permission of the State Historical Society of Wisconsin.

Wisconsin sampler.
1. Wisconsin - Social life and customs - Addresses, essays, lectures. 2. Wisconsin - Biography - Addresses, essays, lectures. I. McCoy, Sue.
F581.5.W57 1983   306'.09775   83-13501

Library of Congress Catalog Card Number: 83-13501

ISBN 0-942-802-03-9

Table of Contents

————————◆————————

i

Preface

———————◆———————

M ost of the yarns in this book are memories — of lumber camps and butcher shops, jitneys and Model Ts; of postmen and pearl divers, carnival barkers and berry pickers; of teachers and preachers, healers and wheeler-dealers. Stitched together like a piece of needlework, they embroider the fabric of everyday life in another time.

Some of the stories herein were originally submitted to Gen Lewis of the University of Wisconsin-Extension's Yarns of Yesteryear contest, whose assistance I gratefully acknowledge.

Sue E. McCoy
August, 1983

■■■

10:10 Lullaby

Blanche B. Lindblad

The creak of the century-old rocker mates with an old woman's bones. She dreams, and it's yesteryear, and she's a child — reliving a simple, better time. There are no words like *ecology* or *Women's Lib.* "Neat" isn't a superlative; it means long stockings, pulled tightly. There's no fuel shortage; the round stove belches soft coal smoke.

Grandma is wanted, needed — for mending, peeling tomatoes, advising. Electric gadgets don't exist, nor food additives. Women are covered; men swear some, chew plug tobacco, and admire.

A depot child, the old lady remembers. Sanborn, Wisconsin. The D.S.S. & A. Railroad, like the Northern Pacific and Omaha lines, was part of a developing north country in the Lake Superior region. The logging industry flourished. Like Grimm's *Fairy Tales* or Lydia Pinkham, the Hind's Lumber Company was a *name*. So was Rust-Owen. The camps, she remembers — the virgin timber in the Drummond-Barnes area — camps and lumberjacks, gaiety in the saloon next door. Immense loads of logs floating by, square stacks of lumber by the tracks. In and out of her dream, white winter peace...

1

Sanborn, a small American melting pot in the Marengo Valley. Surrounding farms of Finnish people in the hills, friendly Croats — with only a mud trail from their Argo location, Iowans, Germans, others. A close community; ladies from the M.E. Church and St. Ann's attending both Aids. Farmers exchanging wares for supplies at the store. A school, a hotel with a pump. Later, the railroad, the depot — a life center. Dad, as agent, transferred from Superior because he craved land, carving out a home on his wild eighty with a canthook and dynamite and a saw.

Clocks were set by incoming trains. Mail in gray bags, cream cans hoisted aboard from large wagons. Telegrams clicking through Dad's fingers, the wall phone cranked. Tickets, information, a dusty smell. People, making connections, invited to eat. Father Sharron, bushy-haired, brilliant, taking five eggs in ten bites. Mischa Elman, polite. Smiling folk, with time to talk.

Trains — fascinating, whistling, churning. Boxcars with bums, cargo-laden flatcars, diners, sleepers with faces. Brakemen, conductors in blue suits approving Mother's Pass. The sound, "Boar—ed!" Lanterns swinging. Rides in the engine, caboose. Trains to crawl under, jump between. Section men pumping handcars. Best of all, the 10:10 night train, rocking a child's bed... An old one feels, hears the lullaby...

The depot, rusty red, had cinders around it and they hurt bare feet. So did the wooden walk leading to the post office. Upstairs, a home. Varnish over paint, portieres draped. In the parlor, a green Morris chair; over the Adam Schaaf piano, a picture; "Frightened Horses." A skirted orange crate for a dressing table, a chammy skin for powdering. Mother, a woman of great beauty, dignity. A curling iron...

Music... The hand-wound phonograph and Galli-Curci. "Once again, once again...I will sing..." An older sister, in plaid taffeta, playing. Mother's soft alto on Stephen Foster airs. Songs from her childhood, Civil War melodies. Stories. Mother's father saying, "Children, royal blood flows in your veins — you are descendants of England's queen, and of Lord North." Mother's mother gathering the family for prayer; her father lining them up against the wall, for straight backs, and saying, "March!" The framed Declaration of Independence, two signers checked with pencil.

July Fourth! The town waking to Dad's firecrackers. A ball game, with homemade outfits. A band Dad secured, playing all day and into the evening until boarding a train for Nabagamon. A little girl, wearing medallions from her mother's wedding suit, forgetting her lines at the flag raising. Men proud, hats removed. Heads up, singing, "And this be our motto: In God is our trust!"

Stability. Surety... The old 10:10... No man's heart failing him, for fear... A coyote, loud, nearby, but not threatening... The train, rocking a bed...

Seasons... Summer, and a swinging bridge over the Marengo River. Summer and the Campfire Girls. Rainbow trout, in a tub. Walking rails, picking strawberries along the grade, dodging snakes. Boulders, sand, heat, bog, bees. Grandview and Delta country, and fat berry pies. Butter from the hills, a lady calling, "Whao!" beneath her orange umbrella. Jumping from a barn beam to hay. Catching fireflies. Cream, fresh bread, brown sugar. Honey in the comb. Laddie-dog.

Work — honorable. Slops to haul downstairs, water from a pump. Night jars to the outdoor toilet, trying not to inhale. Milk from a neighbor, daily in the dark, avoiding the rain barrel. The lawn swing, creaking, swaying; listening to night sounds. People dancing at Woodman Hall, its floor corn-meal clean...

Fall. School, and a mother always waiting. Sateen bloomers and a new middy suit. Learning, loving poetry: "By the shores of Gitchie Gaumie..." The exciting traveling library, small art prints. Respect for a teacher with a horsewhip.

Blazing Birch Lake maples. Cottage cheese curdling on the black range. Dad working his cabbage cutter, for kraut. Dill pickles weighed from a barrel, cookies by the pound. Games. "Happy is the miller, who lives by the Dee." *Burning,* inside, when that boy's hand touched...

Winter was Christmas. An orange and a Hershey bar in a stocking; gifts from a rich aunt... Lanterns on the snow, crunching feet. A school program, with sheets for curtains.

A frozen buck in the warehouse, above freight; coal scuttles with papers beneath. Icy water pails. Breath-on-air in the bedrooms, heavy quilts with cotton bats. Buckwheat pancakes, from a sour starter, on chilly mornings. Boiling beef with onions, chicken stew, biscuits.

Mother doing applique. Mother in a beaver coat — pelts trapped by Dad. Dad, in black half-sleeves, shaving lumber in his office, for a sled. The millpond, pre-tested. Bonfires, clamp-on skates, shadows, mystery. Sore throats, and a swab of blue vitriol; turpentine and lard on the outside, and a sock. Dr. Andrus, from Ashland, in his sleigh.

Holiday dinners, with napkin rings, and Rogers Brothers silverware, 1847. A sister tatting. Folding long underwear around ankles. Flannel slips, angels in the snow. Long evenings. Dad, a history lover, recounting a nation's course. Puff-puffing, Standard tobacco in his pipe. Tales of his boyhood in lower Michigan. Working in a sawmill for a few pennies a day. Training for telegraphy. A honeymoon ride in a caboose... Reading, trimming the lamp wick...

Magical spring. Apple blossoms, wet feet. A shoe box of paper

3

dolls, lost to the wind. Arbutus. A garden, hand-wrung clothes on the line. Sugar cookies, pieplant sauce. Dandelion greens. Violets and cowslips, and tomboy tricks at dusk. Dad at White River, fishing suckers; little fingers in the spurting holes of a water pipeline...

Easter, and church. A jacketed stove. A thumb, wet, turning Bible pages. The pump organ; a deep voice singing, "They crucified my Saviour..."

Remembering... A crowd. Listening to Teddy Roosevelt. A great man. *He was President!* World War I; the Flu; a child sensing the start of global tragedy. Woodrow Wilson, in a tall hat, long coat. A little sister atop a red chair, entertaining — singing, "O how I hate to get up in the *mawning.*" People of good will, clapping. Alert, looking clean... The smoke of the D.S.S. & A. absorbed by blue skies...

Absolutes; God, Country. People looking ahead: A marching pride, a "God Bless America" in hearts. A peace present; wisdom overshadowing knowledge. Dedication. Washingtons and Lincolns in overalls, at farm chores — and tapping out messages in depots.

A child's hand outstretched, eyes solemn. "I pledge allegiance..." A child, blessed — each night, train-trundled. The 10:10 lullaby of yesteryear. Rocking, an old lady remembers, and dreams...

■■■

Sword Swallowing

Gertrude McGaffin

W hen Mother remarried after Father died I had my first experience with carnival life. My step-sister and her husband had several illusion acts with the Castle & Hirsch Shows. When the carnival came to our hometown my step-sister needed someone to take her place while she visited relatives. A friend and I were asked if we could fill in while the show was in town. We were 14 and our answer was an enthusiastic "Yes!". We knew nothing about how illusions were done so it was fascinating to learn the secrets of such tricks as "The Three-Legged Woman," "Being Sawed in Half," "Having a Head Without a Body" and "A Body Without a Head." These were among some of the most memorable illusions we two girls worked and almost before we knew it, it was time for the carnival to move on. Then, joy of joy, we were allowed to go along with the carnival to Detroit. But in September it was back to books and studies and several years elapsed before I returned to carnival life.

It was at the end of a touring season that I again became involved in my relatives' illusion show. They wintered in the South and rented vacant stores where they put on their shows. Typical of so many carnival shows of that time, they had their so-called "Freaks of Nature," such as the Fish Man, whose body was covered with fishlike scales that dropped off as he walked. His ears were just slits in the sides of his head, and he had no eyelids. My first sight of him was quite a shock. There was a Popeye the Sailor Man and a variety of other acts such as a Fire Eater, a Sword Swallower, and a number of small tricks and illusions.

One winter while working in Memphis, our sword swallower became critically ill and was hospitalized. Advance booking for the show had already been made for Nashville and she was advertised as one of the main attractions. Our publicity agent notified Nashville that our sword swallower would not be there due to illness. The reply we received was blunt: "The act is advertised, people expect to see it and you better have it unless you want the group to go to jail."

We were in a quandary. There were only four women in the show, one of whom was the sword swallower. We three remaining were asked if we wanted to try to swallow swords. I had my doubts about it, so I kept quiet, but the other two were sure they could learn and were eager to try. They didn't last long, though, as they became hysterical when they tried. That left me. My brother-in-law had me begin with an ordinary steel table knife with blunted edges. I had less than a week to succeed in the endeavor. The first time I tried, I tipped my head back and held the knife over my open mouth, but I was shaking so hard that the knife just swayed back and forth over my open mouth like a pendulum. The other performers kept encouraging me and after some good-natured needling I succeeded in swallowing the knife.

Within a few days I progressed to a regular sword and by the time we did our show in Nashville, no one was the wiser that I wasn't the "real" lady sword swallower who had been touted in the show bills. With each show we did I became more adept at the trick and my brother-in-law decided to add something new. He had a neon sword made which was 14 inches long from hilt to tip, and lit up inside my chest, producing an eerie glow. It was quite sensational and was the start of my role as the featured sword swallower.

■■■

Doc Kerscher

as told to George Gambsky and Jill Weber Dean

I t was on February 19, 1885, that my behind was slapped and
I yelled my greeting to the world. A greeting no different,
I suppose, from all the greetings I have heard as I slapped
more than five thousand newly born behinds. The first thirty-five
hundred greetings joyously filled homes; the remainder echoed about
hospitals.

Perhaps the man with the greatest influence on me in my boyhood
years was Euren's doctor. Probably because none of his sons showed
the slightest interest in medicine, he took a great interest in me. Often
he allowed me to drive him about in his horse and buggy when he
went to tend to the sick and injured. Even as a boy, I was interested
in the ailments and injuries of people. I helped set many broken arms
and legs before I was fourteen years old.

When I was fourteen, my father purchased a farm fifteen miles
outside of Euren. I worked on that farm for nearly a year, and then
I got a job as a clerk in a store. After three years of clerking, I took
my savings and enrolled at Oshkosh Normal. Oshkosh Normal would
not make me a doctor, but it could make me a teacher, and that seemed
to be the best I could hope for.

In 1907, I received my teaching certificate and returned to Euren
as a schoolteacher. After three years I had saved enough money to
go to Marquette University School of Medicine. My strongest memories
of medical school are not of the nearly sixty hours that I put in studying
each week, but of the dissection classes. No matter how carefully we
washed our hands to rid them of the formaldehyde, the evening meal
had a preserved taste about it.

I graduated from Marquette in 1914 and immediately took the state
exam. It was the last year in which Wisconsin would license a doctor
without requiring him to serve an internship. I did it! I was twenty-
nine years old, and now I could begin to practice medicine.

On June 29, 1914, I married my childhood sweetheart, Helen
Bott'kol, and a week later I hung my shingle in Euren. In those days,
doctors were everywhere. It seemed that all someone had to do was
whistle and several would come running. That first year was a rough

one, and many a meal came from a little creek nearby with brook trout in it. I'd wait around the house until noon, hoping that someone would want my services. If no one wanted me, I'd go to the creek and fish for our supper. From the creek I could see a window in our house, and, should someone want me, Helen would signal by hanging a white sheet in that window.

In 1914 a country doctor's success depended as much on the number of babies he delivered as it did on everything else he treated. During my first year, I delivered only six. In later years I delivered as many as 180.

The practice of medicine in those early years was different from what it is now. There were no telephones, no cars, and no paved roads. The doctor was expected to make house calls, which he did by horse and buggy. For every patient that came to my office, I saw ten more in their homes.

I never did much surgery. I'd sew up wounds, set broken bones, tape ribs, remove cysts, even pull teeth. Whenever I diagnosed that surgery or other extensive treatment was necessary, I referred the patient to a hospital, like Bellin Hospital in Green Bay. The doctor it was named for was my teacher in first grade.

Things are a lot different now. The infectious diseases are almost extinct. Flu epidemics today are mere shadows of what they were when I began in 1914. The epidemic of 1918 was terrible, with many deaths. All of those miracle drugs and all of those marvelous instruments that doctors have today make it possible for them to help in ways that we couldn't even dream of then. It's not all a change for the better, though, because of what's happened to people. Now they eat too much, drink too much, smoke too much, and they exercise far too little. Everyone is too impatient today, and such carrying on doesn't make for a long, healthy life.

When Helen died in 1954, I decided to slow down a bit. Now I hold office hours only from around seven in the morning till nine at night. Sixty-three years have convinced me that medicine is a combination of knowledge, personality, and the faith of the patient in the doctor. Schools supply the principles, but it is experience that supplies the education.

■■■

Frenchie's Ghost

Muriel J. Berger

The summer of 1908 had been an unusually hot one, and this July day had been no exception. I sat on the steps in the darkening evening, the concrete cool against my back. My brother Robbie sat next to me, unusually quiet for a noisy seven-year-old. It was that magic time when crickets and frogs, and all the other night noises drown out the sounds of the day. The fireflies' lights were just beginning to hover over the south meadow, and they seemed to dance on the tips of the grass. A cool breeze moved tentatively over our sticky skins now and then, keeping off, temporarily at least, the hoard of mosquitoes that would eventually engulf us, driving us indoors.

My dusty, bare toes twisted delightedly in the cool, deep grass where the dew had already begun to form. And, as I leaned back against the top step and gazed up at the brilliantly sparkling sky, I heard the sound of hurrying feet crunching along the gravel of the Marsh Road coming from Grand Rapids. Pa heard it too, and he looked at Ma who sat in the big rocker next to Pa's on the front porch of our new brick house.

"Old man LeClaire go to town today?" Pa asked.

"I think he left early this morning," Ma noted.

"Had plenty of time to do his business then," Pa observed, "and, I suppose, to fortify himself for the walk home, too."

Pa talked this way because he thought Robbie and I wouldn't understand about Mr. LeClaire's fondness for drinking.

When we went to town to trade produce for the staples that we couldn't grow on our farm, we took the team. It was an all-day treat for all of us. But Mr. LeClaire took his team only when he needed to take oats or a load of wool to trade. On those occasions when he wanted to spend a few hours with his cronies in one of the saloons that lined the streets of either community, he walked the eight miles to Grand Rapids or the four miles to Rudolph.

Ma's brief smile flashed in the dying light. As the sound of Mr. LeClaire came closer, a delicious shiver of anticipated fear slid down my back. When Mr. LeClaire came he brought with him a whole world of shadowy figures that could strike terror into the hearts of Robbie and me. Yet, as always, we could hardly wait for whatever tale he would tell. I guess it was because Mr. LeClaire was so unshakeable in his belief that he really did see the things he told us about.

As the sounds neared, the steps slowed, and the figure of Mr. LeClaire emerged from the growing dusk. He was a short, wiry little man, with not a pound of spare flesh. Pa said that was because he was forever hurrying to keep ahead of the "something" that always seemed to chase him on his lonely walks home from the saloons. He was the father of a brood of eight children, all married or gone except the youngest daughter. He and his wife lived in the farmhouse across the road from us, and he often visited us upon his return from his trips to town. Perhaps he was more sure of his welcome here than he was from his often irritated wife.

It was the trading he did that brought the cash to spend for the bottle Mr. LeClaire usually kept hidden in his haymow. He changed its location periodically to outwit his wife, Marie, who objected strenuously to drinking.

Tonight he approached from the south. The walk from Grand Rapids was a lonely one over miles of flat, marshy land. There were almost no houses along the road to break the loneliness. For his sixty years, his steps had been hurried and he was short of breath. We knew Mr. LeClaire had encountered "something" again on his trip home.

Pa's pipe glowed as he lit it, and let out a cloud of smoke. "Have a chair, John," Pa said, giving Mr. LeClaire a chance to catch his breath. Pa continued, "Nice day, wasn't it? Did you check on the price they were paying for eggs? Clara has nearly a full crate in the cellar."

Robbie and I squirmed impatiently through a brief discussion of eggs, butter, and new potatoes. We could tell that Mr. LeClaire was

10

eager to get on to another subject, but Pa tried to keep him from talking about it. Grownups can be so irritating sometimes!

We caught our breaths as we heard Mr. LeClaire say, "Noticed it again tonight, Robert."

"Oh, maybe you were just tired..."

"Are you saying I just imagine things? Or, like Marie, you think I spent too much time in the saloon before I started home? It's not true, you know. I know what I saw. It was almost like the other time at the camp. I told you about that, didn't I?"

We held our breath, hoping Pa wouldn't say yes. It was one of our favorite stories. But, Pa, after a quick side glance at Ma, merely said, "I'm not sure."

"Don't you remember?" Mr. LeClaire paused to light his pipe now that he had his breath back. We wiggled with anticipation. "It was a couple of years ago when we were logging Grandfather Falls. It was the first year I was there, the time Frenchie got knifed in that card game.

"They were sitting there around the stove, playing cards. They weren't supposed to do that, you know. It was against the rules. But, it was late in the season, almost time to go home, and the men weren't paying too much attention to rules anymore. Then angry voices started shouting. There was a lot of pushing and hitting and with so many fists and elbows flying, we were never sure who pulled the knife. The next thing we knew, Frenchie was lying on the floor, blood running, the knife sticking from his chest.

"The boss heard the noise, and came running to the bunkhouse. But it was too late. Nobody could save him. He died, and no one knew who did it. And Frenchie will never rest until he finds his killer. He'll keep after all of us until he gets the right one!

"A few weeks later, the roads became too muddy for the oxen to drag the sleds down to the river, and the boss decided to shut down for the summer. Everyone left except me and Emory Prost. We stayed on to close up camp."

Logging camps provided winter employment for many of the farmers in our area. When winter broke and the river opened, the logs started their journey to St. Louis. Then the farmers were free to go home to work their farms for the spring and summer. But sometimes, someone had to stay for a few days to tie up loose ends. An indifferent farmer, Mr. LeClaire was the perfect candidate to delay returning to the farm, except for his problem. He usually saw "something," which made him pack up and leave, work done or not.

"Well, we had just closed up all the buildings, and were planning on leaving the next day ourselves. Emory had a bottle in his things, and we had just had a drink or two before we turned in to our bunks.

11

That's when it began — the weird noises, the screams. I tell you it was awful. We lay frozen in our bunks too scared to move. Finally we got up and went to the window. And then we saw it! There was a glow of strange, blue light off in the woods. I tell you, I don't know how long that thing out there kept us from moving, but we just stood there and stared. Then another scream ending in a long wail tore through the stillness, and our legs finally remembered how to move. We both jumped back into our bunks, neither of us daring to speak, the quilts over our heads. When it was light we went out where the light had been, and there, on that stump, was blood, still fresh and sticky. I tell you, it didn't take us long to pack up and leave...."

There was a long silence when no one dared to speak. Then Pa's reasonable, calm voice said, "John, I've seen lights in the woods, too. But, it's nothing to be afraid of. It's just the glow found around rotting wood." It was the same explanation Pa always had at this point in the story.

"But the blood, Robert. Rotting trees don't have fresh blood. And the screams?"

"An owl may have killed a rabbit."

"You can think owls and rabbits if you want, but I knowed it and so did Emory. It was Frenchie coming back and dying again. He wants to find his killer, and he'll take back any one of us with him. It must be lonely lying up there in that woods alone..."

Pa's quiet voice shattered the stillness, and we all jumped. We had heard this story before. But at each fresh telling, Robbie's and my doubts about Pa's theories grew stronger and stronger. Now, Pa's quiet logic never penetrated our terror.

"But, what's that to do with tonight? Surely, the ghost of Frenchie, if such a thing exists, didn't follow you here to Rudolph from way up north?"

"I don't know. I only know what I saw and heard. And I heard him again tonight!"

"Robert, the children—" Ma's voice broke in. Ma thought Mr. LeClaire was a bad influence on Robbie and me. We held our breaths. We just *couldn't* go to bed now!

"Please, Ma, we aren't tired. Let us stay up a bit longer."

"Well, I suppose..."

"Oh, let them stay," Pa said, and we settled back again, letting the fear wash over us anew.

Mr. LeClaire leaned forward, the long-dead pipe held in his hand, his elbows on his knees. He continued as if he had not been interrupted.

"I left Grand Rapids early, and it was just getting dark when I got to the Marsh Road. As I walked along, I began to see a light, way off across the marsh. As the night grew darker, the light grew brighter, and it seemed to be coming nearer. And then I heard it! I knowed it was Frenchie coming to get me! It was that same chilling cry. I'd know it anywhere. So I started to run.''

Mr. LeClaire seemed to get more breathless again as he recalled the terror. And that same terror grabbed at Robbie and me.

"Well, I got to the stone quarry hill, you know, by the brickyard, and I was getting pretty tired. Just then, I heard another sound, like a horse running. As I got to the top of the hill the horse appeared. I was tired, and I figured if I could catch that horse I could ride it home. I looked at it again, and it didn't look right, almost as if you could see through it! But I decided to grab at it anyway. Just as I reached out for it I heard that scream again. Then it hit me! This was Frenchie's old white mare coming to take me back to Frenchie! So I let go and she up and disappeared just like that. I didn't stay around, I tell you. I just came on here as fast as I could.''

Pa sighed, "Now, John.''

"Don't tell me about owls again. What about the horse?''

"That could have been Schmick's old gray mare. She could have jumped the fence. She usually does, you know. And she'd look white in the dark.''

"Well, you can say what you like, but I know what I know. It was Frenchie's mare, no doubt in my mind.''

Mr. LeClaire sounded stubborn as he slapped at the mosquitoes that had begun to descend on us during his recital. He rose from his chair, and he started down the steps. With a cautious glance toward the stone quarry hill, he started across the road as if he expected Frenchie to be following him again. Pa stood up, too.

"And it's time for you young ones to be in bed,'' Ma broke the spell of silence.

"Upstairs? Could we have the lamp tonight? Please, Ma, we'll be careful.'' Robbie almost knew what the answer would be, but he had to ask.

"Now, you know how I feel about lamps upstairs with you young ones alone. You get to fooling around, anything could happen. They're too dangerous, and besides, oil is expensive.'' But, moved by the fear she heard in Robbie's voice, Ma relented. "I'll take one up for you if you hurry.''

We hurried up the stairs, taking care not to go near the south window. It was as if Frenchie might be hovering there, having lost Mr. LeClaire for the time being.

"Aw, Ma, can't you leave the lamp a while,'' Robbie begged as she started to leave and her shadow grew large and menacing on the wall.

"Now you know there is no such thing as ghosts. Go to sleep or

13

the next time you'll have to go to bed before John gets you all riled up."

"Of course we don't believe in ghosts," I quickly assured her. "Go to sleep, Robbie, and don't be a baby."

As she left the room, my brother whispered, "I know that there aren't any ghosts, really — are there?"

"Course not," I said, trying to make my voice sound convincing. After all, I was nine, and I had to maintain that superiority. "Now, go to sleep."

"Could we look out the window, down the road toward the stone quarry hill, just to make sure?"

I considered it for a moment, waves of fright coming over me again.

"Don't be dumb, Robbie."

"Please, just once, so I can go to sleep."

The decision was difficult. If I said no, Robbie might start to cry, and we would surely be sent to bed the next time. But fear pulled at me, too. Finally, Robbie won out.

"All right. But just for a minute."

We crept to the south window and peered out. As we gazed out into the now darkened night, off in the distance we saw a faint, but definite, glow way out across Mosquito Creek. Neither of us had to say a word. It was old Frenchie, coming across the bridge just this side of the hill. He was coming this way!

We dashed back into bed. Although the night was warm, we pulled the quilt over our heads and held each other tightly. We knew Mr. LeClaire had to be right. We had seen it, too. Frenchie's ghost was real!

■■■

When Milkweed
Went to War

Louise Shartle Coleman

I n July 1944, in the midst of World War II, Wisconsin 4-H members received an eight-page folder with their copy of the *Wisconsin 4-H Leader*. "Your country's armed services need milkweed floss," it declared. It described the plant, explained how and when it was to be collected and stored, and concluded with these stirring words: "School children of America! Help save your fathers', brothers', and neighbors' lives by collecting milkweed pods."

The wartime heroics of Wisconsin youngsters grew out of the dust-bowl years of the 1930s. That was when an immigrant to the United States, a former Russian Army surgeon named Morris Berkman, began studying milkweed. Berkman measured and weighed and tested every part of the plant, including the fluff. And because of this fluff, the fortunes of milkweed took an intriguing turn that involved the United States Department of Agriculture, the War Production Board, and hundreds of thousands of rural children in Wisconsin and other northeastern states.

Before entering World War II, America was importing ten thousand tons of kapok from the island of Java each year. The kapok was used as stuffing for mattresses, seat cushions, and life vests. With trade in the South China Sea interrupted by the war, a substitute for kapok had to be found, especially for filling life vests.

Berkman's studies showed that the silky hairs of the milkweed seed were in fact hollow cells. A life vest containing twenty-two ounces of milkweed fluff would support a grown man in water for four days. The fluff did not compress when confined in a small space. Neither did it mildew, an important feature in a war being fought in the tropics. It was suggested that milkweed floss be used as insulation in flying suits as well. The sheepskin jackets worn by pilots in unheated cockpits became lead weights when the men were forced to bail out into the water.

In the meantime, Wisconsinite Charles Frederick Burgess had done research on what he called typha, the fuzz from the cattail plant. Burgess argued that typha had advantages over milkweed down. Because it only grew in marshy, untillable land, the cattail did not compete with cash crops. And unlike milkweed pods, which had to be picked when the seeds ripened in the fall, typha could be gathered well into the winter, an important consideration when labor was scarce and every hand was needed at harvesttime.

But the War Production Board, upon advice from the Department of Agriculture, chose milkweed fluff as the substitute and set up a pod separation plant in Petosky, Michigan, in 1943.

It took about two large onion bags containing eight hundred pods apiece to fill one life vest. The goal established for Wisconsin youngsters was 50,000 bags of pods. But when the state's Agricultural Extension Service made its annual report, it noted that Wisconsin children had collected the staggering sum of 283,000 bags of milkweed pods in the fall of 1944.

Plans were being made to grow milkweed commercially, but by late summer of 1945, both the war with Japan and the love affair with the milkweed plant were over. There was no further need for milkweed floss when trade with Java was reestablished. In the late 1940s, the introduction of man-made fibers made even kapok obsolete. Milkweed was left to compete with thistles, goatsbeard, and velvetleaf. But with the increasing scarcity of petroleum and carbon-based fibers, who knows? Milkweed may serve its country yet again.

■■■

The Beast
That Will Not Die

Gerald Carlstein

F rom Egypt's Valley of the Kings to the upper reaches of the Wisconsin River runs a thread of fact and fancy that, in the late 1800s, captured people's imaginations, attracted (or so it is said) the scientific curiosity of the famed Smithsonian Institution, and whetted the pecuniary thirst of the world-famous P.T. Barnum. The object of all this attention was a foul-smelling, horned monster that came to be known as the Black Hodag of Rhinelander.

The story — to call it a tale might insinuate a lack of veracity — began on a summer evening in 1896. It was the heyday of logging on the upper Wisconsin River, and Rhinelander was not precisely what one would call a family town. It was exactly the kind of environment, however, that could — and did — give birth to a hodag.

The father of the hodag, or at least the first man to report seeing one, was Eugene S. Shepard. He had arrived on the scene in 1870, when Rhinelander was a tiny trading community called Pelican Rapids, situated where the Wisconsin and Pelican rivers merge. Shepard was later known as a naturalist, but most records indicate that at the outset, at least, he was a timber cruiser. Shepard also admitted to being a cook, compass man, canoe man, and beast of burden. Some say he was also one of the super pranksters of all time.

Out for a stroll that fateful evening, Shepard afterwards related that the first indication of the hodag was its smell. Different reports call the odor strange or weird. One colorful recounting termed it a stench as bad as a combination of buzzard meat and skunk perfume, but that may have been an exaggeration. All versions seem to agree, however, that the aroma was unpleasantly distinctive.

At any event, there in front of him, Shepard saw an animal almost three feet high and some seven feet long. It was covered with black hair. A pair of horns grew from its head. The beast had glowing green eyes, and a dozen sharp projections protruded from a back that sloped like that of a giant lizard. The disagreeable fumes seemed to spew from its flaming red nostrils. Tusks thrust downward menacingly from the corners of a vicious mouth. Its short, thick legs were tipped with elongated needle-sharp claws.

17

Shepard immediately summoned a group of nearby lumberjacks, who fearlessly helped him trail the creature to a cave. Using a sponge soaked in chloroform and attached to a thirty-foot pole, the group ultimately captured the odoriferous animal and hauled it on a logging sled to Shepard's home. Taking no chances, Shepard incarcerated it in a pit measuring thirty feet in depth and fifty feet in diameter.

Shepard's scientific knowledge then came into full play. After studying the fearsome beast, he identified it as the missing link between the ichthyosaur and the mylodon. The animal was also found to resemble a strange creature described by one of King Tut's hunters and recorded on a scrap of parchment that had been found in Tut's sarcophagus. A reporter from the staff of the *New North* newspaper translated the Egyptian word *selblatkey* into "hodag."

One hodag story indicates that a female hodag was also captured, along with a baker's dozen eggs, which later hatched. However, no more was heard of the female or any of her offspring.

Never reluctant to turn a dollar, Shepard exhibited his hodag at the Marathon, Langlade, Lincoln, and Oneida county fairs from 1900 to 1903. In his book *Badger Saints and Sinners,* Fred L. Holmes states that "interested writers from the east and Smithsonian scientists came to view the beast." Another source claims that P.T. Barnum indicated an interest in the creature.

Sometime later, Shepard "confessed" that the creature was a hoax. He said that his hodag had been carved from wood and then covered with hides. The horns and spikes and tusks, said Shepard, were bulls' horns. Steel rods were used to shape the formidable claws. That's what he *said*. But what is fact, and what is fiction? Newspaper accounts cannot be located. The Smithsonian archives, supposedly complete, make no mention of the hodag. If P.T. Barnum was interested in the beast, no documentation of such an interest remains. And if Shepard had any records or proof of the creature's existence, the materials were probably lost when his home was destroyed by fire, in 1908.

But consider some other legendary creatures: the Loch Ness monster, the Abominable Snowman, the Bigfoot. Written accounts of reported sightings are available, but the descriptions detailing the appearance or size or habits of these as yet uncaptured species are always the same. Such mindless repetition of vital statistics, as though the facts were committed to memory, causes one to doubt the truth of the stories. The existence of such creatures becomes suspect.

Not so with the hodag. In one account, for example, the hodag is the size of a rhinoceros and has body hair a mottled color. That doesn't sound much like Shepard's moderately sized hodag. Could he have captured a baby? Was there more than one sighting?

The original version of the hodag legend tells of the lumberjacks watching the beast eating turtles, clams, and snakes. Shepard said the hodag ate white bulldogs exclusively, and those only on Sunday. This was obviously a jest. Other hodag stories claim that beef cattle and other domestic animals were the beast's favorite food. As a result of these tales, there was a drive to exterminate the hodag. Is it possible that Shepard embellished the facts about his discovery and then concocted a "confession" to protect a nearly extinct species? All we know is that in 1903 the hodag disappeared from sight.

The memory of the beast lives on in Rhinelander, however. The town is known as the home of the hodag. The football team is called the Hodags. One of the top winter snowmobile races, the Hodag 50, is held annually in Rhinelander. A three-dimensional, full-size model of the hodag is displayed in a glass enclosure at the logging museum in Rhinelander's Pioneer Park.

If you ever get up Rhinelander way, keep your camera handy. When you're out in the woods for a stroll some evening, you just might catch a glimpse of the long-lost Black Hodag. But don't be frightened. Unless, of course, it happens to be Sunday and you are walking a white bulldog.

■■■

Lumberjills

Linda Myer

L egend says that the flapjacks were bigger than platters, the griddle so vast that four men greased it by skating across on hogs strapped to snowshoes. The cook is usually described as a burly man with thick moustache and forearms like tree limbs. Reality paints a different picture. Sometimes the figure flipping the pancakes was a woman. Though women are not a part of logging-camp folklore, they went "a-logging" all the same.

Before 1890, Wisconsin lumberjacks hacked away at the edge of a wooded wilderness. Logging camps were all-male societies in which bigness and toughness were supreme values. It is said that because "only the toughest could survive," the camps "produced...veritable hellions — rough, tough, lusty and thirsty...whose only pleasures were booze, bawds, and battle." They had no homes, only rough-hewn, lice-infested bunkhouses, and were as transient as the rushing rivers on which they drove the logs to market in spring.

As the lumber industry pushed westward, leaving behind great swaths of cleared land, an army of settlers came to farm the cutover. They brought with them to the frontier all the accoutrements of civilization — plows, dishes, churches, saloons, and schools. Some of these settlers obtained jobs in logging camps to earn cash for their farms. As a quieter, more stable class of men began to replace the Paul Bunyans, the character of the camps began to change; they became more settled and homey.

The arrival of women in the camps accelerated this "civilizing" process. Transient lumberjacks, who previously had known only bar-maids and prostitutes, came into contact with women who wanted to marry and settle down. Even rough-mannered loggers spoke more politely and engaged in fewer fights in the presence of women and children. Most of the loggers were protective of the children and en-joyed making toys for them and teaching them woods lore.

Most women joined logging camps to make money, often so they and their husbands could more quickly acquire enough cash to buy a farm. Some couples, already settled on farms, needed cash for tools, taxes, supplies, or emergencies. Esther Gibbs, of Spooner, became a camp cook to earn money for her two-year-old son's operation.

Money, however, was not the only reason women worked in the camps. Some wanted to keep their families together. Mary Padjen, whose husband was hired as camp cook, took a job as part-time kit-chen helper, or "cookee," because she was reluctant about being left alone with a young baby.

Married women were hired as cooks and cookees, never for woods jobs. Unmarried women were allowed only as members of the cook's family or as assistants to a female cook.

What was camp life like for these women? The cookshack, a long rectangular building, was the center of their universe, the place where they worked and lived. Early cookshacks were made of logs. After 1920, they were nothing but cheap boards covered with tar paper. To reduce heat loss, there were few windows. The floor was made of rough planks. Cracks provided drainage when the floor was scrubbed, a convenient but very drafty arrangement. Aina Nyman, who was a cook in a camp near Ironwood, Michigan, remembers that her hundred-pound sacks of flour used to freeze to the walls.

Quarters for the cook and her family were usually just bunks in the kitchen. A blanket draped in front of the bunks provided the only privacy. In a few camps, small bedrooms were built onto the cookshack wall — a real luxury. Nails on the wall served as closets; blankets were thrown over the clothes to protect them from flour dust and grease smells.

Sylvia Niemi, who worked as cookee for her mother, once found a more private place, but her stay was brief. A married couple had built a cabin near the cookshack, but they left camp unexpectedly, aban-doning the cabin. "So," recalls Sylvia, "I fixed it all up. I brought all my clothes in there and slept one night. I was scared stiff! Then I went outside and saw a big bear. I hauled all my clothes back into the cookshack!''

Dining tables filled one end of the cookshack. At the other end was the kitchen. It was unlike any household kitchen. Everything was on a giant scale and arranged for efficiency. Typically, the two wood-burning cookstoves were eight feet wide and had thirty-pail caldrons attached by pipes to the fireboxes to supply plenty of hot water. There were racks above the stoves for drying pans and dishes. Flanking the stoves were work tables for rolling out pie, bread, and cookie dough. Above them were cooling racks for baked goods.

The person overseeing the whole production, the cook, was the single most important person in camp, including the foreman. George Corrigan, an ex-foreman, explained, "If you didn't have a good cook, you didn't have anybody." Wages for lumberjacks were small, but decent meals could compensate for a lot.

Where food was concerned, quantity was as important as quality. Esther Gibbs, a cook near Hayward, regularly served a "family" of sixty. One day's meat might be half a hog, a quarter of beef, or a hundred pounds of weiners. Sometimes she would stretch out the meat with a keg of pork sausage. Reported Esther: "Twenty-five pounds of lard, 25 pounds of navy beans, a bushel of potatoes, 50 pounds of flour, 15 to 20 pies, a bushel of cookies and doughnuts, 6 to 8 gallons of vegetables, 25 pounds of tea, 10 pounds of oleo, 25 pounds of white sugar, 25 pounds of brown sugar. . . . These were the staples day in and day out. There were raisins, rice, macaroni, dried apples used here and there too."

Preparation of these enormous meals was usually executed by one cook. In camps with fewer than thirty men, she did the cleanup and service, too, though in larger camps cookees were hired for such tasks. Supplies came in only once a week, ingredients were sometimes unavailable, and refrigeration was impossible. In addition, it was the cook's job to keep daily food costs within a strict budget of about fifty cents per person. However, a cook who could serve tasty food promptly three times a day despite these limitations was in great demand and earned two or three times more than the average lumberjack. During the Depression, cooks' wages ranged from a low of thirty-five dollars a month to as high as one hundred dollars a month. Room and board were always included.

The cook earned every cent. Typically, she arose at 3:00 a.m., lit the fires in the cookstoves, and mixed pancake batter in washtubs. She would fry hundreds of pancakes on long cast-iron griddles, stash them in the oven, and proceed to fry sausages, doughnuts, and potatoes. At 5:30 a.m., the men filed in. Tables were laden with serving bowls

22

of each dish. The cookees scurried between tables and kitchen, refilling bowls and coffee cups. The men ate in silence and quickly left for the cuttings. The cookees cleared the tables, washed the dishes, and reset the tables. The cook, meanwhile, was hard at work on the next meal. Sylvia Niemi remembers her mother's labors: "Right after breakfast, she'd start making pies. She'd make ten, twenty pies a day. And biscuits and cake and bread. And she made cookies all the time....She worked all day long." Such was the daily routine. The cook rarely hung up apron and spatula until nine or ten in the evening.

Though this work load was no different for male cooks, many female cooks also had to find time to care for their children. Sometimes a woman went to her own or her parents' home to deliver, but occasionally babies were born right in the cookshack. Alex Kurki's mother told him that he was born "between dinner and supper." The foreman would choose a substitute cook from among the other crew members or simply add cookees to the kitchen staff until the mother could return to work. Nonetheless, there were many months when a new mother had to fit feeding and diapering into her busy schedule. Children learned to amuse themselves and to do kitchen chores very early.

Evening leisure time was fairly quiet. Esther Gibbs remarked, "At night, when those fellas came in, they were ready to fall in those ol' bunks." People talked, told stories, and sang. Often, the younger men chatted with the kitchen girls while helping them peel the next day's potatoes. The women also read, knit, crocheted, and embroidered in their spare time. The daughter of one cook remembered wearing slips that her mother made from flour sacks. They had four inches of crocheted lace at the top and bottom.

Before the late twenties, transportation in the northwoods was slow and difficult, so people remained in camp most of the time. Although the loggers often went home or to town on Sundays, the cook and cookees could not leave because they had to feed all who remained in camp. Sunday was not a holiday for the kitchen crew, but it was an easier day because there were fewer to feed.

With improvements in transportation came greater mobility. Passenger trains ran daily between Bessemer, Mellen, Ashland, and Duluth. It was possible to hop the train in the morning and go shopping, visit a friend, have a beer, and return by nightfall. Even in their few hours off, the kitchen staff could go somewhere and return in time to serve the next meal. When cars and trucks proliferated, in the mid thirties, social life in the northwoods bloomed. "I didn't stay at camp very much in the evenings," said Sylvia Niemi, who was a sixteen-year-old cookee in 1936. "The young fellas there, they'd have a car. Well, we'd bunch up and go to dances....We'd pick up my girlfriends on the way." There were dances several nights a week in neighboring towns like Ironwood, Bessemer, and Iron Belt. Battery radios were available, too, and Sylvia recalled listening to Major Bowes' Original Amateur Hour and Fibber McGee and Molly.

Eventually, the camps were populated largely by people from the surrounding farms, people who had known each other for years and shared family and community ties. Logging camps were no longer isolated enclaves housing a "different breed" of men, but became instead an integral part of the northern farming communities. And while the camps were changing in character, they were also becoming fewer in number. By degrees, the large tracts of timber were decimated. The big camps themselves finally became part of northwoods folklore, along with river drives and two-man saws.

As the heyday of the lumbering era came to an end in Wisconsin, the land began to cover its scars with second-growth timber. The burly lumberjacks became the subject of song and story. The women, few in number, were not heralded as folk heroes. Yet, in helping to tame the wilderness, they left their own indelible mark on the northwoods.

■ ■ ■

In My
Not-So-Merry Overland

George A. Richard, Jr.

B ack when clocks seemed to run in low gear, the loudest noise most folks heard was Fourth of July firecrackers or the furious chugging of 2½ horsepower gasoline engines. Into this comparative bliss came a new noise: the putting and belching of that terror of horses, the automobile.

One of the many makes manufactured in those days was the Overland. It was an ideal family car for those of modest means. It was simply a two-seat, four-door convertible. With Mother, the smaller children and the ever-present grandma seated in the back, Dad and the older children would take to the front and the family would be off to visit some unsuspecting relative. In our town, Overlands were sold by Genesee and Lammert. Genesee was a native of New York state and well-to-do. Lammert was the son of German migrants of modest affluence. Dignity was his middle name.

In those halcyon days just before World War I, it was the practice of auto dealers to drive out into the country to make sales to the farmers. Part of the deal was that upon delivery of the tin lizzy the dealer would give the purchaser a lesson in driving. It was just such a day one spring when Lammert decided to take a spin out to see a possible customer. The snow was gone, but so were the road bottoms.

Before leaving town Lammert dressed to the nines, derby atop his head, and put up the top of the Overland, having seen a few clouds in the distance through his gold-rimmed pince-nez which were always perched on his very Roman nose. Nothing pleased Lammert more than to be seen behind the enormous wooden steering wheel of an Overland. As he left town that day he was particularly proud of himself and he saluted friends and neighbors right and left. Out into the countryside the Overland chugged. Like a ship rolling in the sea, the vehicle rocked along through potholes and mud. Lammert quickly perceived that the roads away from town were in impossible condition. But, with Teutonic stubborness, he snugged his derby down firmly, adjusted his pince-nez, and pressed on. Then it happened.

In the middle of the road was a pothole large enough for a middle-sized porker to take a Saturday night bath. It was surrounded by other potholes that *looked* worse, but actually were nothing compared to this particular pothole. Lammert proceeded to take the middle ground. There was a bang as the vehicle lurched across the muck-hole, and Lammert was propelled upwards like a projectile through the cloth top. As luck would have it, Lammert at this precise moment was passing through a small settlement. The sound of his machine had broken the stillness of the spring day, bringing the usual sampling of curious to the doors and windows of the saloon and store. What they saw was truly unforgettable: an automobile bouncing along the road with a man's derby-bedecked head protruding through the roof. The head was turning this way and that, screaming something in German. When Lammert's head went through the car top, the back of his neck and his chin were forced in between the braces which held the top up. The car kept going because there was no foot-feed, but instead a lever on the steering column which controlled the fuel flow. No doubt Lammert was wishing his mother had given birth to a four-armed son, because he needed two arms to free his head and two to bring the vehicle to a halt.

In the end fortune smiled upon our salesman. The Overland careened along until it came to a low ditch, at which point the engine simply killed. Lammert freed himself and tried to regain his composure. Ignoring the group of spectators about him, he removed the derby, its crown crushed and its brim dangling from his neck. Bent but not broken, the pince-nez were replaced upon the Lammert proboscis. Starting the Overland, Lammert mounted his place behind the steering wheel like a king ascending his throne and drove off slowly with as much dignity as he could muster.

The excitement over, the grownups returned to their beer and talk over the war in Europe while the young folks resumed their play, most of them unaware that this quiet spring day was but the calm before the storm. How could these tillers of the earth know that in a few moments of history's clock they and their world would be swept away forever in a brutal war, the Roaring Twenties, and the Great Depression? Or that Lammert's noisy vehicle was but a whisper of what was to come.

■ ■ ■

P.H. Kasper – By Himself

❖

I was born in the Town of Rhine, Sheboygan County, October 11, 1866. From early childhood I was greatly interested in cows and young stock, so I had full charge of them as long as I remained at home. Work on the farm was done almost entirely without aid of machinery, and the days were long. There were meager returns for our milk hauled to the cheese factory — about fifty or sixty cents per hundred.

While waiting for a job as a country store clerk, an incident occurred which changed the entire trend of my thinking and doing. I was aroused from sleep one midnight by the son of our local cheesemaker, who had driven over the two miles of rough, hilly road to urge me to come to work in the cheese factory, as he was going away. The father operated the farm and the mother made cheese. She had instructed him that he must get Phillip Kasper to come and help her.

The factory had been sadly neglected, but the work there appealed to me. I thought I had the finest position in the world. I knew how to scrub — I had helped with the housework at home, and my mother had impressed upon me the importance of cleanliness and order. So I washed and scoured the inside of that factory and the utensils until everything was shining. I still remember the man who patted me on the back and said, "My boy, if you keep this up you will be a real cheesemaker some day, and you will never be without a job." And I never was.

In those days the factories were in operation only during the summer months, and in the winter I was able to attend school. During the summers of 1885 and 1886 I worked on an eighty-five-acre farm beside a cheese factory. My work lasted from four o'clock in the morning until nine o'clock at night. I wanted to feel that I was earning my compensation of thirteen dollars per month. The second season I got a raise, to twenty-six dollars a month.

After that I worked for several years making cheese in Sheboygan County, but the farmers there wanted quantity, while my ambition was to make *quality* cheese. But it requires more milk to make *high quality cheese* than it does to make just cheese. I also made cheese in Cobb

27

for a few years, and then I went to Raymond, Minnesota, for fifty dollars a month with board, room, and work for the entire year.

I found the cheese factory still under construction. No machinery had arrived. I then said that I would go to Sioux Falls, South Dakota, for a visit with my brother and that when the machinery arrived they might wire me at my expense.

In a few days a telegram to return arrived. But to my confusion, there was an eight-horsepower boiler instead of the self-heating kind to which I was accustomed. All I know about a boiler I learned that first day. Working by lantern light we finished the job late that night. The milk was strained into the vat after we were done, and cooled. The next day we added the morning's milk and we were all set to make cheese.

As I made cheese that day, the Stuarts' relatives were notified and they came from Willmar, twenty-two miles away, to witness the process. Finally the cheese was made and put in the press. Two hours later supper was announced and I was asked to bring some cheese for the table. When I said the cheese would not be ready to eat for ten days, there was a family consultation. They doubted that I knew how to make cheese, and I was told not to start a fire in the boiler the next day unless I received notice from Willmar to go ahead.

At Willmar there were two businessmen from Sheboygan. One operated a meat market, the other a furniture store, but they knew cheese. So they were consulted. That night Robert Stuart, who was managing the farm for his brothers, received a telegram, and came to me with a beaming face. "Start your fire and make cheese," he announced. All the milk from one hundred cows was in the vat, and the cheese I made that day I thought was the very best I had made in six years of experience.

May 8, 1891, I opened my present factory for business. It was like all other cheese factories in those days, single boarded, eighteen by thirty-six by twelve feet, a partition in the center, one part for making cheese, the other for a curing room. Cheese hoops and a rake for stirring were the only equipment. In my first season here, 1892, I made seventeen thousand pounds of cheese. Now, in the sunset period of life, I look back and take inventory of my achievements, content that I have been able to contribute something to the great cheese industry.

I feel that I owe a large measure of my success to my beloved wife, a native of this vicinity, who stood by me during the lean, uphill years, encouraging me and making our home a place of rest and good cheer.

During the fifty years in which I have operated my own factory, I have passed on to others the essentials of good cheesemaking. Many of the outstanding cheesemakers in Wisconsin received their training

in my factory; this realization is a source of pride and satisfaction to me.
—Excerpted from *The Golden Jubilee of the World's Champion Cheesemaker*, May 1941.

■ ■ ■

Guides of Yesteryear

Mel Ellis

T he old-time guide, tough as a hardwood knot, was a crack shot, expert trapper, skilled angler, superb boatman, and discerning woodsman. But none of this was what made him truly special. What set him apart more than anything else was the fact that he considered his guests as friends first and customers only second.

Things have changed, of course, and as more and more guides come north from city streets instead of emerging from the brush, the vacationer may feel as if he is a faceless fisherman rather than a guide's companion and confidant. This is neither a condemnation of the modern guide nor an attempt to elevate to sainthood the guide of yesteryear. It is no fault of today's guide that there are more and more customers going after less and less game. And if yesterday's guide was likely to be more knowledgeable about nature, he was just as likely, come supper, to pick deer hair out of the stew with one finger while stirring coffee with the other.

But just as yesterday, with its patina of misty mornings and rose-colored sunsets, seems more beautiful in retrospect than anything nature can produce this instant, so, too, the recollection of old-time guides stirs nostalgic memories.

Who is there today to compare with the indomitable John LaRoc, guide to presidents, who even in his eighties could pole a long boat *against* the boisterous current of the Brule River? In what wilderness hideaway can you find another George Ruegger, of whom the late Ernest Swift said, "I would not trade three days of grouse hunting with George for a whole winter in Florida. He gives dignity to hunting..."? Where is there another Banty "Red Shirt" Brandt, equally the scourge of deer, muskies, and legislators? In what county is there a Fred Minor, a warden and sometime guide, whom Governor Robert Lennon of Louisiana described as "A rare man!"? Where is the man to match Johnny Helsing, who, with a single dog and a sandwich, could walk a wolf to death?

Strictly speaking, most of the old-timers were not really guides at all. They were resort operators, trappers, woodsmen, fire-tower watchers, who might take a man fishing or hunting if they took a fancy to the way he stagged his pants. Even the purely professional guide (if there ever was such an animal in Wisconsin) had to supplement his income from guiding with any odd job a rigorous north country might provide, or risk going hungry.

Not surprisingly, some of Wisconsin's greatest guides were conservation wardens who took time off to introduce celebrities to the wonders of Wisconsin. D.W. "Bill" Waggoner was an example of these warden-guides. He was a tough warden one minute and a gracious host the next. His experiences guiding an astounding array of famous visitors were as unusual as his experiences enforcing the fish and game laws. Bill was guiding Gypsy Rose Lee, for example, when she was still electrifying Broadway audiences. Gypsy caught a muskie, and in her excitement started an impromptu striptease. Bill got her sweater to prove it. Then there was Julius "Cap" Krug, a Democrat and former Secretary of Interior, who compared the biting habits of muskies with the tactics of members of the Republican party. Bill guided slugger Ted Williams of the Boston Red Sox, too. "Hardest working man I ever saw," he recalled. "Caught eighteen muskies on one trip and released them all."

Five Eisenhower brothers gave Bill his worst case of jitters. "The muskies hadn't been hitting," Bill explained. "We'd been out the day before the Eisenhowers were due to arrive to see if there was anything we could raise them on, and we couldn't get a nibble. Thought sure when they got here we wouldn't be able to show them a good time, but believe it or not, on the first day, each of the brothers caught his muskie."

Bill was embarrassed while hosting Kentucky's Acting Governor Weatherby. He had to tell the Governor that Wisconsin didn't issue complimentary licenses, and that he'd have to buy one. Weatherby looked at Bill and the Vilas County countryside around them and said, "The cost of a license is, indeed, a small price to pay for the privilege of fishing in such magnificent country as you have here." And that was only the beginning. Bill guided Matt Auslinger, then head of the United States Bureau of Narcotics; John Martin, Wisconsin Supreme Court Justice; Andreas Feininger and Wallace Kirkland, *Life* photographers; John Carradine, movie star; and a score of others who went away convinced that Wisconsin, besides having great hunting and fishing and great scenery, had some of the finest guides in the world.

Of course, not all guides were as affable as Bill Waggoner. Red Shirt Brandt was a five-foot firebrand. If the fish weren't biting, his guest would get a lesson in conservation he'd never forget. Always attired in a flaming red shirt, Banty Brandt tackled governors or millionaires, compatriots or enemies, with the same explosive verve.

Almost without exception, the guides of yesterday came from a long line of men who had met and conquered the challenge of the un-compromising north. If they seemed hard-bitten at times, so might any man who had to stretch a can of beans into a week's provender. I came late to the world of guides. Many of them were already old when, in stiff new boots, I came north. Others lived only as legends, but sitting around a campfire with a son or a grandson, I heard it all once more — how they came out of the woods to meet the trains with buckboards, drove their guests over rutted roads, and housed them in primitive log cabins built without a single nail.

In those days, a good guide was expected to feed his customers, entertain them, guard them, keep them comfortable, and sometimes even tuck them into bed. He lighted their cigarettes, tied on their lures, took off their fish, and occasionally even carried their guns when the snow got too deep. Some good guides still wait on customers hand and foot while afield, but once off the water or out of the woods, the sportsman usually is expected to fend for himself.

Still, guides are like apples. They're not all good. In the course of hunting and fishing all over the Americas, I've had guides by the hundreds. Some were Indians who couldn't find their way out of the woods. Some were white men who couldn't start their own outboards. The average, however, was excellent, and nowhere were there any better guides than those who taught me to revere Wisconsin. They are still to be found, too, men firmly grounded in outdoor lore, but with a flair for using up-to-the-minute innovations. I remember Laurence Ellerman of Star Lake, who began guiding when he was seventeen. When I visited him some years ago, he was combining all the tradition of the good old days with the mechanized wonders that

32

have taken most of the sweat out of hunting and fishing. And any northern Wisconsin sportsman could add to the list.

Sometimes, though, looking back, I try to decide which guide was the greatest of them all. I never arrive at a satisfactory answer, because where one could hit a running deer with open sights at one hundred yards, another could boat a muskie a day without fail. Where one knew the names of every flower and bird in the woods, another made the best "slum-gully" this side of heaven. Where one could entertain me with inspiring stories of the days before the big timber came down, another could quote poetry by the ream.

Personally, the men who boated the Brule were my first and most enduring idols. Of these, John LaRoc (guide to presidents Hoover and Coolidge) stood head and shoulders above the others. He made his own boats, knew every stone in the stream, stood straight going down the fastest rapids, edged a craft so the angler could slip a fly under any overhanging bough, and loved every sentinel pine, every blueberry, every grain of sand of his beautiful valley.

A man half his age, a schoolteacher named Lawrence Berube, stands out next in my memory. A protege of LaRoc's, Berube was also a naturalist, carpenter, hunter, and now-and-then guide. Berube was one of the best fly fishermen I ever knew, and he held *Field and Stream* records for his big rainbow trout, but what made him most attractive as a guide was the way he identified with the land. He was no alien creature trespassing; he was a part of the forest like a deer, a part of the river like a rainbow trout.

Lake Michigan and Lake Superior ports had (and still have) their special deep-water guides, men who knew all about the way a wind can sweep an unsuspecting skipper to his doom. One of these, Harold Thorp, grandson of one of the first resort operators in the state, tried to quit but couldn't. After retiring, he went to Florida, but before long he returned to his beloved Fish Creek to take customers, each summer, out among the Strawberry Islands for bass, trout, perch, and salmon.

Some memorable guides, like Frank Jackson, started out as farmers. The Jacksons got to feeding and caring for so many fishermen that they finally let the plow rust and began operating a resort in 1900. A heavy ledger records their story. Frayed and yellowing, it is an heroic account of hard work. Entries tell of buying bacon at sixteen cents a pound to feed fishermen who wrote, "Caught a whole boatload of pike." When Frank died, the business went to his son, George, and when George died, it went to *his* son, Art. The family moved to Little St. Germain, leaving the cabins behind, but taking with them the fine sense of responsibility that pioneer resort operators and guides had for their friends, who just happened to be their customers.

33

Of course, there still are guides like the Jacksons left in the state. They still wear stagged, woolen pants, and even if they're mainly resort operators, they guide whenever they can. But like the wolf, they are becoming a rare breed. Yet even though the old-time guides have largely disappeared, the stories about them still live. And around Brule they tell of the time when woodsman Gilbert Jorgenson all but sawed off his leg, and then after a wild ride to Superior, lost it anyway. Guide Lawrence Berube came to the hospital to give a quart of blood. When Jorgenson regained consciousness, Berube said, "Well, you old Scandinavian, how does it feel to have a Frenchman's blood in your veins?" And despite his loss, Jorgenson could laugh.

The old-time guides were like that. They became the friends of thousands, and their lives were the stuff from which legends are made.

■ ■ ■

Tree of Candles

Melba Baehr

O ur Christmas tree was never trimmed with anything but candles — dozens and dozens of wax candles. We never strung popcorn and cranberries, never made paper chains, never used tinsel or colored glass balls. Just candles.

For years, until electric lights replaced wax tapers, whenever I saw candles on a tree they reminded me of the Christmas tree we had when I was a child, and what each candle stood for. The Tree of Candles was a tradition in our family, one that taught a lesson.

All of us children were expected to give "gifts" at Christmas time that were presented with no expectation of a gift in return. Every time we gave a gift we were allowed to select a candle to be placed on the tree. There was keen competition among us to see who could contribute the most candles. Mama would say, "I don't want to see an inch of tree by Christmas Day. I want to see nothing but candles."

The first day in December, Mama set out boxes of wax candles of assorted colors. But long before December rolled around we had been busy thinking of gifts to give. Perhaps that is what Mama had in mind, wanting us to do good all year round, and not just at Christmas time. At any rate, the result was that we were kept busy most of the year, thinking up things to do for others and ways in which to share with them. The joy this gave us made us want to do something nice for someone else.

By mid-December, when Papa cut the tree, we had quite a number of candles ready to go on its boughs. We inserted our candles in metal candleholders and clamped them on the branches of the blue spruce. I always favored red candles, though the choice was a difficult one to make, for other colors sometimes seemed equally attractive.

Our gifts were not all the kind that could be purchased at the general store or made at home. A gift could be something helpful done for another, or a thoughtful or kind act. We were all expected to give, from the oldest child to the very youngest, who could learn a bit of recitation to tell to an elderly person, or perhaps save enough pennies for an orange to present to a neighbor. The older girls knitted woolen mufflers and shawls. The boys carved toys from wood and made little wooden carts for children who might have no other toys at Christmas. When the first snow of the winter fell, we began our snow-shoveling service for widows and elderly couples. Sometimes a gift was as simple as saving an apple from lunch and taking it to a lonely shut-in on the way home from school. As often as not, it was the visit that was the real gift, whether there was an apple to give or not.

Papa donated a ham from the smokehouse or a sack of potatoes to families in the neighborhood who were having difficulty making ends meet. Mama made cookies and loaves of bread for their Christmas dinners. All of these were gifts, and every time we reported a gift to Mama she smiled proudly, and looked on happily as we selected a candle.

It was surprising how many things we could find to do when we really set our hearts and minds to work. "Two candles are better than one," Mama would say, "and ten are even better." And so the candles multiplied during the month of December.

On Christmas Eve we all gathered around the tree while Papa, using almost a whole boxful of matches, lighted all the candles. It was a glittering sight and, together with the scent of the blue spruce, our home was filled with the mingled, aromatic aroma of wax and evergreen, and the joy that comes from sharing.

A candle, like a good deed, sheds light in the world. Many candles shed more light than one. So it is with kind, thoughtful acts. That is the lesson taught by the Tree of Candles.

■■■

Free and Clean

Charles F. Church

T hey still stand in farmyards around Wisconsin, creaky old ghosts with rusted arms. Once they drew water for the farmer's home and for his stock; now they trellis morning glories or hold up the television antenna that draws in Madison or Green Bay. In winter, against gray skies, they look like bare trees yet hold no promise of renewal. They signify not just pages gone from the calendar but a way of life that has gone from the countryside. Windmills are relics come back to haunt us from the days of cheap energy and self-reliance.

It was the windmill, not the Colt revolver, that really won the West. Windmills turned cattlemen from nomads into ranchers, brought water to homes and towns on the prairies, and filled the boilers of steam engines that linked a sprawling nation by rail. The first American windmills, patterned after Dutch machines, were too huge and unwieldy to transport. Then in 1854, Connecticut machinist Daniel Halladay patented his Standard, the prototype of subsequent windmills. It had a sectional, spring-loaded, wooden wheel that folded up in strong gusts instead of blowing apart, as a Dutch-style mill would if its canvas sails were not furled. And the Standard was small and simple enough to be shipped from the factory and assembled on the site.

Halladay had taken out his patent halfheartedly, wondering how big the market would be for his device. But as wave after wave of settlers went west and homesteaded farther and farther from preempted rivers and streams, demand surged for machinery to raise the ground water that could now be tapped by newly developed percussion drills. By 1860 windmill manufacturing was booming, and Halladay moved his company to Batavia, Illinois, to be closer to the burgeoning market.

In 1867 Leonard Wheeler, a missionary to Indians and trappers in some of the wildest reaches of Wisconsin — Madeline Island and the mainland settlement of Odanah — patented a windmill with a solid wheel and a tail vane that turned it out of too-severe winds. Wheeler's sons set up a factory (the precursor of Fairbanks Morse) in Beloit, and their Eclipse windmill became the Standard's chief competitor.

Then in 1888 Thomas D. Perry, a former Halladay employee and a pioneer aerodynamics engineer, and LaVerne Noyes, a farm equipment manufacturer, combined their talents to develop the Aermotor, the first practical steel windmill. Perry designed its curved sheet-steel sails to meet the wind at a pitch calculated to derive optimum power. Reduction gearing made the Aermotor smooth running and so efficient that it would pump water in a breeze that would not even turn the wheel of a wooden mill. In subsequent years the Chicago-based Aermotor Company offered such refinements as an all-steel tower that tilted down to provide easy access for oiling the gears, and galvanized wheels and towers for rust protection and good looks. Within a few years, the mass-produced, back-geared Aermotor had captured eighty percent of the market.

"Since the advent of the Aermotor," a sales agent's bulletin of 1894 proclaimed, "other windmill manufacturers have not known what to do except to do the thing we do, and their thoughts and energies have been paralyzed through fear of what we might do next." Indeed, in the 1905 Sears, Roebuck catalog, a mill strongly resembling the Aermotor was offered as the "Kenwood Back Geared Galvanized Steel Pumping Windmill." An eight-foot mill could be ordered for less than twenty dollars, and a twenty-foot tower cost less than fifteen.

By 1929 nearly one hundred companies were manufacturing windmills in what had become a ten-million-dollar-a-year industry. Then the Depression struck. And soon after, the Rural Electrification Administration began making good its promise to bring cheap electric power to every farm in America. As country people began installing water systems that filled their sinks and bathtubs and even their stock tanks at the turn of a tap, most windmill companies that had survived the Depression got out of the business. Two or three small companies produce windmills in America, and Aermotors are still being made, though the factory has moved to Argentina.

Today in the countryside hundreds of windmill wheels turn aimlessly in the wind, their parched gears and bearings creaking, their dangling shafts bobbing uselessly up and down. It would be comforting to think, in these times of dwindling energy resources, that a windmill revival is just around the corner — but it isn't. Even the biggest farm windmills put out no more than one-third horsepower under ideal conditions, not enough to run a pressurized domestic water system.

Once these machines gave us the power of the wind, free and clean. Then we demanded more than they could give. Now the wind is master again. And when farmers wake in the night and listen for the windmill's lulling, rhythmic squeak, all they hear is the chuckling breeze. But though they may fall from their proud towers, old windmills never die; they just fade into a calendar landscape of America's used-to-be.

■■■

Paul Bunyan's Cookbook

Alonzo W. Pond

Part I

There are many published accounts about Paul Bunyan and his famous loggers. The facts of his exploits in the great forests from Maine to Oregon have been well described by able authors in books, pamphlets, and magazine articles. It would be presumptuous of me to try to add anything to the luster of Bunyana except for the lucky break that brought a hitherto undiscovered manuscript to my attention.

A few years ago I met Charlie Boyd at a Lakeland-area fair. Charlie has lived up here since the time main roads detoured around old pine stumps so big that Paul Bunyan himself didn't bother to pull them out of the way. (Some folks claim he didn't need to remove the stumps because the snow got so deep the dray could slide right over the tops of the biggest ones.)

"I'd like to have seen a load of those big logs," I told Charlie.

"They say the smallest was as big as the MacArthur Pine over near Laona. Did you ever see a really *big* load, Charlie?"

"Yes," he said. "You could, too, if you're any good at skin diving."

"How would that help?" I asked.

"You remember the time Paul had a wagonload of beans break through the ice on Bean Soup Lake just before the spring drive began?"

"Yes," I answered. "There wasn't time to get in another shipment, so Paul piled slashings around the lake and kept fires going until the water boiled and cooked the beans."

"That's the time I mean," Charlie said. "Cooked a lot of *big* fish as well as the beans. When the drive started, Paul dug a canal from Bean Soup Lake to the river and sluiced the bean soup down to the river pigs. The men said they didn't mind having to drink so much water to get a taste of beans, but they objected to the soup's fishy flavor.

"That's the sinking you often hear about," Charlie continued, "but there was another; a load of logs was sunk. You know that lake near the Tomahawk River, just off Highway 70 west of Minocqua?"

"Where the river flows north for three miles and then makes a big loop and flows back south?" I asked.

"That's the place," said Charlie. "Well, the Tomahawk River is really Paul Bunyan's Round River. When he logged off the Pyramid Forty, the logs just rolled down to the river. But when the drive began in the spring, the men couldn't understand why it took so long to get to the mill towns. Finally, Shot Gunderson, the best log spinner in Paul's camp, recognized a peeled log caught on the shore. 'That's the log I spun the bark off the first day of the drive,' he said. 'We been going round that hill for twenty days. We're on a round river.'

"Everybody knows about the Round River drive," Charlie continued, "but not everyone knows that it made Paul so mad he planted dynamite all around the hill and blew it right off the map. Round River was straightened into the shape of an old-fashioned hairpin, and right where the old Pyramid Forty was, the blast made a small, deep lake. The lake's bout halfway between the north-flowing and south-flowing channels of the river.

"Two years after Paul had cleared the Pyramid Forty, he logged east of the river. No use making a six-mile river drive, Paul figured, when they could skid across the little lake to the south-flowing channel. All went well until the last load. That last load was the biggest. There were single logs seven feet thick. Witnesses said the two bunk logs were eight feet ten and a quarter inches and nine feet two and a half inches, respectively. They were a mite inclined to exaggerate, though, being over thirty.

"It *was* a big load, though. Even Paul was impressed. He sent for an artist to make a picture. There's a man standing close for scale, and if he was a normal logger, say six feet one without his boots, that load towered up well over seventy feet! Of course I've heard it said the artist used a midget for a scale and that the load wasn't more than fifty-three feet. Anyway, at the last minute Johnny Inkslinger, the only one of Paul Bunyan's crew who could write, came out of the office with a big roll of birchbark under his arm.

"Paul said, 'What you got there, Johnny?'

" 'That's my chef d'oeuvre,' said Johnny. 'It's the record of all the supplies we've bought, all the menus the cook has served, and all the recipes he's used. It even includes notes on the special occasions for some of those meals. I want it to ride on this load — the biggest haul ever made out of this camp.'

"With that speech, Johnny tucked his birchbark manuscript among the logs. It was no problem to get the load moving. It was so big its weight melted the ice underneath the runners — just like a glacier — so a little tug from the team set the mass in motion. The logs moved majestically out onto Short-Cut Lake. It was later in the season than Paul thought, however. The lake was still frozen over, all right, but spring weather had softened the ice. As the load left the shore and moved out onto the ice, there was a long, rumbling roll of sound — the kind you get in early winter when the thickening ice is adjusting to the contracting cold.

" 'Watch it!' shouted Paul to the swampers walking on each side of the team.

" 'Step lively, boys,' the teamster said to his big Clydesdales. There was a loud, sharp crack. Another long rumble. Then another, and another.

" 'Cut loose the team!' shouted Paul. 'Cut 'em free!' The two swampers swung their axes at the evener and sheared it clean off as neat as they'd drop a tree limb. Then they ran for shore. Horses and men reached the far bank as the whole surface of Short-Cut Lake broke into fragments and the heavy sleigh with its chained load of logs slid below the surface.

"Now, ordinarily that would have been only a minor accident," Charlie explained, "because white pine — cork pine, loggers call it — floats like a boat. Paul expected the whole load to bob to the surface. Of course, Paul didn't know that when he blasted the Pyramid Forty into oblivion and straightened out the Round River he had also exposed a ledge of Precambrian rock. When the load of logs sank beneath the waters of Short-Cut Lake, it slid right under that ledge. Despite the buoyancy of the logs, the chained load stayed trapped deep below the surface."

Thus ended Charlie's tale. After I heard the story, I stopped at

Bo Popov's sport center and asked about local skin divers. Bo recommended Walter Skinandowski, a student at Lakeland High School. I told Walter that I wanted a report on some old logs on the bottom of Short-Cut Lake. He and I went over there and anchored about where I figured the logs were. Walter found them the second time down.

"Holy cow," he said when he came up after the second dive. "There's a pile of logs down there as big as a church!"

"Work around the ends of the pile and see if you can find anything loose to bring up," I suggested. Walter went down a couple more times and came up with a roll of birchbark.

"It's the only loose thing I could get away from that pile of logs. They're all chained together in a big heap."

"Well, let's quit. This will be good enough for a souvenir," I said. "Maybe I can unroll it."

I paid Walter and went home. It was quite a job to unroll the bark, and it took some weeks of careful museum technique to get it straightened out enough to see the marks on it. In the meantime, Skinandowski moved away, so I couldn't tell him about the interesting manuscript he recovered for me. I hope he reads this and learns that his diving made a small contribution to Bunyana.

Everyone knows that birchbark is indestructible. Fortunately, Johnny Inkslinger had invented a waterproof ink, which he used on that birchbark scroll. His notes are as easy to read today as they were the day they were written. According to Johnny Inkslinger's manuscript, Paul was a great eater but didn't have the patience to be a cook himself. Paul was a marvel at picking the brains of contemporaries in any field that interested him, and being a lover of good food, he naturally consulted the renowned Escoffier of France. From him, Paul absorbed the great principles of food preparation. These Paul passed on to each of his camp's best cooks. At Paul's urging, Escoffier finally published his own cookbook.

If judged by modern standards, some of these accounts seem somewhat exaggerated. Others, I suspect, are just plain lies. Be that as it may, I felt obliged to make this source of authentic new information about such a historic figure as Paul Bunyan available to historians, camp cooks, gourmets, and other readers. For years, however, I was stymied by the monumental difficulties of translating the recipes into the modern jargon of cups, ounces, teaspoons, and tablespoons. Paul's cooks never heard of such trifling measurements. His Muskie Chowder, for example, called for a wagonload of Boston beans, 313 tiger muskies, a spring-fed lake, sixteen shovels of salt, three shovels of pepper, and two oxtails — with heads and bodies attached — to disguise the flavor of the beans.

Muskie Chowder

Step 1

½c. old-fashioned, dried, white beans
2 c. water

Soak beans in water 12 to 24 hours. Cook beans over medium heat until soft, 1½ hours or more. Drain beans. Save bean water. Also save beans.

Step 2

6 oz. tiger muskie filets (or panfish)
2 medium onions, diced
1 bouillion cube
1 c. hot water
1 t. salt

Dissolve bouillion cube in water. Add bean water from Step 1. Add raw fish, onions, and salt. Boil gently until fish and onions are tender, 20 to 25 minutes. Add beans from Step 1.* Simmer a few minutes more. Serves one Wisconsin lumberjack or two average Americans.

*Oxtail Variant

¾ lb. oxtails
2 c. water
½ t. salt

Cook oxtails over low heat until meat falls off bones, about 4 hours. Skim off most grease. Add meat and broth along with beans.

■■■

Part II

P aul Bunyan had a problem at his logging camp. In January he'd ordered Hot Biscuit Slim, the cook, to invent buttermilk flapjacks. "I'll do it," said the cook, "but you'll have to invent maple syrup to go with them. Flapjacks and maple syrup! I'll bet the loggers will eat thousands."

Now it was April, and Paul realized that Hot Biscuit might already have invented the breakfast flapjacks. He knew he had to get busy on the maple syrup. So, as Paul often did when he had a serious problem, he went to visit his Indian friend Bill Catfish, who lived in a comfortable, birchbark wigwam across Powell Marsh from the logging camp.

"I'm going hunting," Bill said when Paul arrived. "You stay for dinner." Bill went over to a big tree and jerked out his tomahawk. When he wasn't using it, he always stuck his tomahawk in the trunk of a tree. That way, nothing would dull its sharp edge. Paul noticed Bill's birchbark canoe was lying right side up directly under the gash that had been made by the tomahawk.

As he wandered around the camp, Paul picked up some branches and carried them to the fire. Bill's wife was getting ready to cook dinner. "We have boiled venison for dinner," she said. "Maybe you get me some fresh water, please, Mr. Bunyan?" Paul picked up a birchbark basket. The corners were folded tight; water wouldn't leak out of it any more than out of a tin pail. He started for the spring. As he walked by the canoe he saw it was half full of clear, fresh water.

"Hey, Mrs. Catfish," he called. "How did this canoe get full of water?"

"It's good water," she said. "Big trees like that always cry when sun gets hot if my Bill cuts one," she said. "It's good water to cook with. Trees cry only on hot days after nights get ice cold."

Paul took a basket of the water back to the fire, and Mrs. Catfish put in pieces of fresh venison. With two sticks she removed hot stones from the fire and carefully dropped them into the basket. The water boiled quickly, and steam rolled up in clouds, giving off a sweet smell. Pretty soon Bill Catfish came home.

"I smelled dinner," he said, "so I got hungry and came home early." Using big wooden spoons, they feasted on chunks of meat and gravy.

"Say, that's the best gravy I ever tasted," said Paul. "I'll bet that would be fine on buttermilk flapjacks. Maybe even better than maple syrup."

"It *is* maple syrup," said Mrs. Catfish. "Your people call the tree that cries in April the maple tree. Its tears get thick when they are boiled. You don't need meat. Just boil the tears till they get thick."

"Can I have the rest of the tears in the canoe?" asked Paul.

"Sure thing," said Bill Catfish. "I'll help you drag it on the snow to your camp. Maybe we wait till night. Then it gets cold. Ice freezes on top. We won't spill any of the tree water."

They hauled the boatload of water to the logging camp. Paul told Hot Biscuit Slim to put it all in big kettles on the stove for the night.

"There's your maple syrup," he said. "It'll be thick like gravy by morning. Have you invented those buttermilk flapjacks yet?"

"No, not yet," Slim replied. "But I'll have them invented by morning." Hot Biscuit Slim was as good as his word. At 5:17 a.m., when Paul walked into the cookshack, Hot Biscuit said, "I've invented the buttermilk recipe as you told me to, Mr. Bunyan. It's going to be an awful job to grease that big griddle and cook those flapjacks fast enough for those hungry loggers, though."

"Three little boys just came into camp on snowshoes," said Paul. "They'd like to work for their breakfast. I'll send them over to help you."

"That's fine," said the cook. "Those boys know how to walk wide on snowshoes. Get 'em here quick. I'll get out six slabs of bacon."

When the boys came, Slim tied a whole slab of fat bacon on each foot and hoisted the lads onto the top of the big stove. "Now don't you kids get lost," he cautioned. "It's just 1,760 steps to the other end of this stove. I want you to walk down the front side and come back on the back side. You've got to swing your weight onto each foot so you leave a good grease spot at each step. You make three spots per second and be back here in twenty minutes."

As soon as the boys set off, Hot Biscuit Slim began pulling on some ropes hanging from a track above the stove. A big hopper with a spout started moving after the three little boys. One kernel of popcorn dropped onto the left side of each grease spot. Another hopper followed closely and poured a pint of flapjack batter on the same spot. A third hopper dropped another popcorn kernel in the middle of the batter.

Well, before those little boys had walked sixteen feet down the hot pancake griddle, the first six popcorn kernels exploded. Six, big, half-cooked flapjacks leaped into the air. Each turned over and landed raw side down, square in the center of the grease spot it had leaped from. By the time the boys were forty-eight feet down the stove, the regular mess boys were racing alongside with long-handled platters, catching the cooked flapjacks as the second popcorn kernel tossed them off the griddle.

In no time at all, there was a regular bucket brigade from cookstove to table. The loggers poured so much new maple syrup onto their plates it looked like Bear Creek flowing down the table. They ate the new buttermilk flapjacks so fast that Hot Biscuit Slim didn't even have time to change the bacon slabs on the little boys. When the last drop of batter hit the stove, he saw that the bacon slabs they had been wearing were fried right down to the rind. If they'd had to grease six more spots, those three boys would have had blisters on their feet.

Buttermilk Flapjacks

1 c. all-purpose white flour
2 t. baking powder
¼ t. baking soda
2 t. sugar
1 egg*
1 c. buttermilk
¼ c. melted shortening
½ t. salt (omit if using bacon fat for shortening)

Heat griddle to 300°-325°. Combine dry ingredients. Beat egg and stir into buttermilk. Add liquid to dry mixture and beat until smooth. Grease griddle. When grease is hot, pour ½ cup batter on griddle for each flapjack. Flip each flapjack when bubbles form on edge. To avoid toughness, turn each flapjack only once.

You can double the recipe without using another egg.

■ ■ ■

46

Part III

Several Bunyan biographies credit Paul with creating the pineapple by crossing the northern thorn-apple with *Pinus strobus.* I have always been skeptical about that claim because thorn-apples — the ones growing along the river of the same name, anyway — seldom have the kind of large, fleshy fruit that characterizes pineapples. Besides, thorn-apples grow best in abandoned clearings and other areas wholly open to the sun. *P. strobus,* on the other hand, grows in towering stands that would shade out any of the little jelly-apple trees that might be close enough to receive wind-borne pollen from the pines.

When I had read my way 137 feet down the birchbark scroll on which Johnny Inkslinger had recorded all the culinary details of Paul Bunyan's lumber camps, I came across the name Jacques Haricot-vert. His occupation was listed as "forester." In parentheses were the words *Jack Beanstalk.* This intrigued me. I read the next several feet of the scroll with extreme care. An underlined weather notation led to proof that Paul did create the pineapple. Like so many other great scientific advances, this one was made by chance. It is now known conclusively, however, that the parent apple trees were not northern thorn-apples, as previously reported, but large, juice-filled apples from the Kickapoo Valley. And despite the accidental origin of the cross-pollination that produced the pineapple, Paul Bunyan deserves full credit for establishing the pineapple industry. Here is the entry from Inkslinger's manuscript:

> Storm with unusual, unpredicted, violent, northeast winds swayed top of regal pine. Pollen-collecting forester clung desperately to slender treetop and saved his life, but the gale twisted the top of his near-full pollen bag into a tight neck. The backlash of the swaying tree snapped the closed bag of pollen from the forester's belt and catapulted it up among the clouds scudding away to the southwest.

Here was an entirely new aspect of Paul Bunyan's omniverous search for knowledge. The fact that one of Paul's foresters was collecting pollen from the top of a giant *Pinus strobus* proves that Paul intended to cross-pollinate selected pine trees to get hardy, fast-growing seedlings for the future production of white-pine lumber. The loss of nearly ninety pounds of *P. strobus* pollen, of course, would have meant the loss of a full year in Bunyan's forest improvement program. That is why I continued to search the manuscript to see if the sack of pollen was ever recovered.

About two feet beyond the windstorm entry I found this: "Torn pollen sack, empty, recovered in Kickapoo Valley. Twenty-three percent to thirty-seven percent failure of Kickapoo apple crop predicted. Poor weather hampered bees before pollination was completed." Obviously, the terrific storm that had nearly blown Jack Beanstalk out of the tall pine and that had carried away his pollen bag had also prevented the Kickapoo bees from fertilizing about a third of the area's apple blossoms.

Paul and Johnny decided to inspect the orchards in person and, according to the manuscript, went to Gays Mills in July. The sheriff of Crawford County recognized Paul. He pulled a plastic bag from his pocket. "Does this belong to you?" he asked. Paul examined the bag carefully. Then he handed it to Johnny, who could decipher the faded printing.

"Pinus strobus pollen. Collector: Forester J. H-V. Bunyan experimental nursery," Johnny read aloud. "It's the bag that was torn away from Jack Beanstalk, all right. His initials were put on with my waterproof ink before he went collecting. That bag had about $87,246.34 worth of white-pine pollen in it," he said sadly, "but it's all gone on the winds of heaven now."

"Well, it will cost you just $200.00, Mr. Bunyan," said the sheriff. "We have an antilitter law here in Crawford County, and I enforce it to the letter."

After settling their fine, Paul and Johnny went on a walk through the orchards. They decided that the estimate of unpollinated trees was not only exaggerated but wholly untrue. The trees wre just as heavy with fruit as they ever were in July. There was one strange fact, however, that had a statistical correlation with the crop-failure estimate. Between twenty-three percent and thirty-seven percent of the fruit was oddly shaped and had sharp, pointed leaves growing out from the end opposite the stem.

Local orchard workers claimed angrily that the deformed fruit was caused by the contents of the torn pine-pollen bag. Paul and Johnny began studying the evidence. An unusual number of green apples had fallen on the ground. Virtually all of the fallen fruit was deformed. The waffle-marked skin and elongated shape of these apples made them re semble pine cones. While Paul and Johnny were pondering the situation, a slight breeze stirred a tree in front of them. There was a shower of dropping fruit. "Look!" exclaimed Johnny. "The falling fruit all lands stem side down!"

Intrigued, Paul asked the orchardist to fence off that particular tree and under no circumstances to allow any disturbance of the windfalls. During the next few weeks, the strangely shaped windfalls grew into large elongated fruits with wafflelike skins and clusters of leaves at the top. Warm weather continued that fall, and the ground-growing apples continued to swell. Early in the autumn, the orchardist sent a couple hundred of the mystery fruits to Paul.

"What are these things?" asked Cream Puff Fatty, the pastry cook. Paul Bunyan just laughed.

"I wish I knew. Maybe they are upside-down apples."

"They look more like big pine cones," said Cream Puff Fatty, slicing one open and cutting a bite-size piece. "They taste all right, though, a slightly sweet, applelike flavor."

"Perhaps a good name would be pineapple," suggested Johnny Inkslinger. "They look like pine cones and taste like apples."

"I don't care what you call them," said Paul, "but see what you can do with them for dessert."

"Sure thing," agreed the chef. "Mr. Bunyan calls them upside-down apples. Mr. Inkslinger says they are pineapples. I'll invent pineapple upside-down cake."

While Cream Puff Fatty was working on the receipt for the new dessert, Paul peeled and ate one of the new objects. It was much juicier than any apple, and the flavor was pleasant. He thought it had great possibilities for commercial development. There was a drawback that worried him, however. Only a few of the thousands of upside-down apples were ripening in the Kickapoo Valley, even though the killing frost was weeks later than usual.

"Too bad your experiment didn't happen in Hawaii," said Johnny Inkslinger. "I think that would be a better climate for the new fruit." Paul concurred. And so pleased was he with his new discovery that he ordered — at considerable personal expense — all the plants dug up and shipped to Hawaii, where they were replanted and grew happily ever after.

Pineapple Upside-Down Cake

Step 1

1½ c. fresh pineapple, diced
4 T. butter
½ c. brown sugar, packed

Peel "waffled" skin from ripe pineapple. Cut into ½-inch slices. Remove tough core. Cut slices into bite-size pieces. Melt butter in 8-inch iron skillet. Stir sugar into butter and heat until syrup starts to bubble. Remove from heat and add diced pineapple. Arrange fruit in single layer in skillet.

Step 2

2 eggs

4 T. + 4 t. sugar
4 T. + 4 t. flour
1 t. vanilla

Separate yolks from whites. Beat yolks well. Beat whites until very stiff. Add sugar gradually to whites. Add yolks to whites. Cut flour into egg mixture with a spatula. Fold in vanilla. Spread cake mix evenly over fruit in skillet. Bake in preheated oven at 400° for 20 minutes. Cake will spring back to the touch when done. To avoid sticking, remove cake from skillet *immediately*. Loosen edges with a knife. Place a plate over skillet. Invert plate and skillet. Lift skillet off cake. Makes 5 lumberjack-size portions.

■■■

Part IV

T he drive was on! Bouncing, shifting, whirling like Saturday-night dancers in the Aragon Ballroom, logs filled the Flambeau River from bank to bank. Paul stood gazing at the rapids-studded, northwoods river. "Beautiful! Beautiful!" exclaimed the great logger as his glance swept westward. Then he turned to his timekeeper, Johnny Inkslinger, and added, "One day we go west, Johnny. We go west to make America strong and big and *magnifique.*" (Sometimes people forget that Paul Bunyan was French-Canadian born. When in the grip of deep emotion, he lapsed into his mother tongue.)

"Certainly, Mr. Bunyan," Johnny replied. "But you still have a little work here in Wisconsin. You've got to get the pine to market *now.* They need houses and stores and warehouses and *saloons* in Chicago and St. Louis and Kansas City. They tell me that since you logged off all the timber in Dakota, farmers are coming in faster than houses can be built. People all over the prairie states are living in *sod huts!* They want houses and barns and churches and schools. You and your loggers are the suppliers of lumber for those buildings. The construction industry depends on *you!*" The intellectual Johnny Inkslinger spoke with great emotion.

"I suppose so," sighed the heroic logger. "I'll keep the pine moving to the mills. I'm glad this drive is riding so high. The way those birlers are working, we'll ride the crest into the Chippewa and on to the Mississippi before you can say 'father-of-waters.' "

Suddenly there was a warning cry from the lookout in the top of General MacArthur White Pine. "Unusual white cloud coming up fast, west-southwest."

Paul turned his gaze in that direction. "Hmmmmmmmm," the logger mused aloud. "The lookout is right. That strange white cloud is a flock of gulls from the Pacific Ocean. I'll bet they've spotted the grasshoppers feeding on Brigham Young's wheat fields."

Just then Jimmy, Paul's messenger boy, came running up to the big logger. "Mr. Bunyan," he yelled, "Mr. Bunyan." (The little boy had to shout twice for his voice to reach the giant's ears. The first shout only got to Paul's belt buckle; the second shout pushed the sound waves on to their destination.)

Paul looked down and saw Jimmy holding up a written note. "Read it to me, sonny," said Paul, who didn't like to admit that he couldn't read.

"I can't. I can't," shouted the lad. "It's classified *top secret!*"

"Bah," said Paul. "I'll bet every bird in the forest knows the

51

contents."

"The pileated woodpecker was tapping it out in Morse code on that big dead pine tree," admitted the messenger, "and I read Morse by ear."

"Give me the contents then, Jimmy."

"From lookout to Paul Bunyan," the boy recited. "Far below and eastward of strange white cloud, earlier reported, is a black — repeat, black — cloudlike mass rolling along the ground. It resembles newsprint rolling out of a Fox River Valley paper mill. It travels east-northeast at estimated speed of five hundred miles per hour."

"I'll bet that dark cloud is a rolling carpet of grasshoppers leaving the wheat fields of Brigham Young. They're probably tumbling over themselves to get away from the seagulls," Paul speculated.

It was just then that Hot Biscuit Slim, Paul's grand chef and master of the cookhouse, appeared out on the river, riding a log. "Look at that Hot Biscuit!" Paul exclaimed. "He's so light on his caulks he could waltz across a chocolate cake without scratching the frosting. I sure lost a wonderful birler when I put him in the kitchen, but he's even better there. Never saw him out for exercise on the drive so near suppertime, though. Must be something important he wants."

The cook danced ashore and looked up at Paul Bunyan. "The drive's going too fast, Mr. Bunyan. There's no meat for supper tonight. The wagon train with forty tons of fresh buffalo tongue is on the way from Kansas, but your logs are moving so fast the wagons can't catch up to us. I need meat for the men, something that will stick to their ribs. You got any suggestions?"

Paul and Johnny Inkslinger and Hot Biscuit Slim walked back to the cookhouse to review the situation. As they were pondering, Joe Mufferau burst in on them. "The Flambeau drive has sunk!" he cried. The four rushed to the riverbank. At the water's edge, they halted in stupified awe. In front of their bulging eyes was a placid stream as docile as an aged river meandering through an English meadow.

"I've seen logjams tame a wild river by backing it up into its floodplain," said Paul, "but this is no logjam. An hour ago this was the wild, rugged, turbulent Flambeau. Now there's not a log in sight."

"You said the drive had sunk," Johnny Inkslinger said to Joe Mufferau. "How do you know? Where is your scientific proof?"

"Come close and look down into the black water," answered the cook's assistant. Big Paul and Johnny Inkslinger looked down. The bed of the river was completely paved with logs.

"But what are those strange shapes on the logs?" asked Paul.

"Grasshoppers," answered Joe. "I looked out here just as the last log sank. It was loaded with grasshoppers. I swear to you that those fat grasshoppers piled onto the pine so thick that the logs got lower and lower in the water until they sank out of sight.''

"There'll be a depression in the bulding industry now for sure,'' predicted Johnny. "Those logs paving the bed of the Flambeau are the finest, straightest-grained timber that ever rode a flood. Now that they are sunk, they'll get waterlogged in a few days and be preserved for posterity as perfectly as the fish found in the Alaskan permafrost and recently served at the annual Explorers Club dinner.''

Paul seemed deep in thought. "Fish,'' he said. "Hmmmmmmmm.'' Then he looked up. "Fishermen tell me that grasshoppers are good bait. With the logs sunk, there's nothing for the driving crew to do. If they can't drive logs, we'll let them drive fish.''

The roar of laughter that met Paul's statement was so loud it was heard in New York. Paul didn't mind the laughter. He told each of the loggers to get a pine branch. He had Johnny study a map of the area and assign every lumberjack to the headwaters of a trout stream. The loggers fanned out over the whole Flambeau watershed: the Manitowish, Bear, Turtle, Nine Mile, Six Mile, and Three Mile. From headwaters to creek mouths, the loggers whipped the trout streams. They drove the rainbows, the brooks, and the browns down to the log-paved Flambeau.

Finally they reached the sunken Flambeau drive. The loggers stopped whipping the stream and went ashore. The tired fish relaxed and discovered the grasshoppers. They sampled the critters and found them delicious. The nourishing food revived the fatigued fish. The trout were hungry enough to eat their weight in bugs and proceeded to do just that. The smaller fish got down between the logs, where the grasshoppers were squeezed in the cracks like caulking filling the chinks of a cabin. A dozen fish working together that way could eat a grasshopper-weighted log free in just twenty-nine minutes.

Before midnight, the logs began popping up to the surface of the Flambeau like bubbles in a glass of champagne. Big Paul woke up and decided to enjoy a moonlight walk along the Flambeau shore. He stopped in his tracks! Logs were popping up in all directions as they were released by the hungry trout feeding on the river bottom. "Slim!'' roared Paul. "The drive is on. Call the men to breakfast.''

Slim asked no questions. He took a deep breath and opened his mouth. His rich tenor voice floated over the river. "Roll out! Roll out, you river pigs. It's daylight in the swamp, and the Flambeau drive is on.'' The call was music to the river pigs. They picked up their peaveys, cant hooks, and pike poles, and they rode the pine to market.

By Friday, the trout were moving sluggishly against the Flambeau current. Even the smallest minnow now weighed about two pounds, and many of the larger fish weighed nearly twenty. The trout were crowded together as thickly as salmon on the spring run. "They're

so fat and lazy now that the griddle boys can catch them by hand,"
Paul said. "We'll have fish for dinner tonight."

And ever since that day, you cannot find a restaurant anywhere in the northwoods that does not serve a fish dinner on Friday night. In addition, the Flambeau River fish drive is ritually reenacted every spring. Thousands of anglers gather on Wisconsin streams and whip the water with ceremonial replicas of the flexible pine branches used by Bunyan's loggers. The withes are now called fly rods, and attached to them are brightly colored feathered imitations of grasshoppers, symbolic of the insects that caused the famous sinking of the Flambeau drive.

Baked Fish a la Flambeau

fish filets, cut into serving-size pieces
corn flakes, crushed
bacon fat, solidified or butter soft

With a knife or spatula, spread bottom of shallow baking pan liberally with bacon fat. Pat fish filets dry. Lay serving-size pieces in pan, spaced so they do not touch each other. Spread bacon fat liberally over each filet. Sprinkle corn flakes over filets. Bake in preheated oven at 350° for about 20 minutes. Fish will be flaky when done. *NOTE: The bacon fat contains enough salt for most epicures.*

■■■

Drummer Boy

Dorothy Blanchard Schmitz

T he lanky figure of a boy was silhouetted in the open window of the band room. I idly watched his bony elbows and wrists beat out a martial strain as he plied his drumsticks on his drum. His long blonde hair fell into his eyes and as he tossed it back with a jerk of his head my thoughts drifted to another place, another time, and to another half-grown lad with a drum. As through a kaleidoscope Joshua Simmons emerged, marching down a narrow and dusty road on a day like this, warm, golden, holding a promise of a long Indian summer. It was October 16th, in the second year of the Revolutionary War.

Joshua proudly beat the drum his father had brought to him from Boston. Born August 8, 1762, Joshua was barely sixteen years old as he marched at the head of the tiny column of enlisted boys and men from his village of Dighton, Massachusetts. They were to join Captain Seth Talbot's company. Word had spread that General Washington was in dire need of reinforcements. Joshua had pleaded with his parents to let him enlist when it all began, but they had stood firm in their refusal until this last appeal. As he often argued, he was the only one left in the village who could play the drum and lead men in a proper march.

Joshua's mother, who had on occasion chased him out to the barn to play that drum, stood with family and friends in the square, wearing her numbness of heart like a mask penetrated by a few tears furtively wiped away as they fell on her cheeks. It wouldn't do to let Josh see her weep, or know of her fears for him. He looked so happy, so proud in his neat homespun uniform, waering those heavy woolen socks she had knitted. News of frozen feet and worn out coats and shoes had reached Dighton. Her Joshua was starting out right with warm new clothes. His long blonde hair was neatly plaited and tied with a red ribbon snatched from his sister's handkerchief box.

All too soon drummer boy Joshua Simmons was a Continental soldier in the War for Independence. All too soon the bright drum was lost beside a ditch and a musket took its place. Private Simmons served in various regiments with the Massachusetts troops under Colonels Hathaway, Sparhawk and Richmond. He was with General George Godfrey's Bristol County Brigade on his third re-enlistment and helped build the fort at Butte Hill. On November 11, 1780, Joshua Simmons was honorably discharged, a seasoned, pensioned soldier, number 14466.

The wind stirred an avalanche of red and gold leaves and a fine powdering of dust rose from the paved street. The school window banged shut. The drummer boy it had framed disappeared, and the daguerreotype vision of my great-great-great-grandfather on that dusty road in Dighton nearly 200 years ago vanished.

■ ■ ■

The Haunting

tales collected by C.W. Orton

T he most famous of all Wisconsin ghosts is the Ridgeway Ghost. Beginning about 1840, this puckish haunt terrorized the countryside between Blue Mounds and Mineral Point. A map was drawn to show the roads around Ridgeway where the spirit was most likely to be encountered, and numerous accounts of the Ghost's mysterious activities have been given.

■ My husband's grandfather had been at a neighbor's all day, and as he was coming home across the fields, all of a sudden he saw this white carriage with two white horses out in an open field. He walked toward it, and then, as he was looking at it, it rose into the air. He ran as fast as he could all the way home. He took to his bed that very night, and about two weeks later he died. In the family they've always said that he died because he saw the Ridgeway Ghost.

■ Four people were walking through the woods, going to some kind of party. It was a clear, calm, moonlit night. You could see almost as well as in the daytime. All of a sudden the leaves whirled up in front of them. There was no wind or breeze or anything. No one was there, but they could see the leaves denting in, as if somebody was walking on them. They just always assumed that it was the Ridgeway Ghost.

■ There was a guy by the name of Willy Powell who had this beautiful sleek team of black horses. He was quite a ladies' man, and he also liked to drink. One Saturday night when he came back home and drove up to the barn, he found the door already open. Standing in the doorway was this huge form, like a man but so much bigger. The horses reared, became untangled of their harness, and away they went. The horses were so petrified that they didn't turn up for two or three days. And I guess old Willy didn't have anything to drink for a while, either.

■ When my mother-in-law was a girl, she saw this light down in the horse barn. She thought maybe her father was in there with a lantern, but when she went up to the barn there wasn't any light and there was nobody there. Yet she said she could feel a presence. She claimed it was the Ridgeway Ghost.

■ The Ghost appeared at a party where they were playing poker, scared the players, and got away with all the money.

■ A fellow by the name of James Ash went to see his sweetheart. On his way home, the Ghost suddenly appeared and walked step by step with him. Neither of them spoke a word all the way, and Jim never went to see the girl again.

■ Back in the 1840s a Welsh miner was trudging along the road just beyond Ridgeway when he suddenly realized he was being closely followed by the notorious Ghost. He quickened his pace, but so did the Ghost. Soon the miner was running faster and faster, the Ghost at his heels. When completely out of breath, the miner slumped down on a log. Mr. Ghost took a seat on the other end of the log. Then the Ghost spoke. "That was some good running you did." "Yes," said the miner, "and I am going to do some more as soon as I catch my breath."

■ Our first child was born in 1959. I got up to give her a 2 a.m. feeding. I'd scrubbed and waxed the kitchen floor that day and had laid some newspapers on it because it had been a rainy day and I didn't want the floor to get tracked up. While I sat in the far room rocking the baby, all of a sudden I heard the kitchen door open. I turned my head and saw the newspapers floating around the kitchen. I could hear steps, but couldn't see anybody. I raced into the bedroom and woke my husband. He listened to the footsteps, now going away. The door closed and that was that. There weren't any tracks on the floor from the dampness of the ground as one might think with the footsteps and all.

■ My husband had a jacket that a girl friend of his had given to him before we were married. About three years after we were married, the jacket disappeared from the nail on the stairway wall where it was always kept. My husband insisted that I had got rid of the jacket. I looked everywhere for the jacket, but I couldn't find it. Then about two or three years later I went into the stairway, and there it was, hanging as it was when last seen — but it was worn out.

Many people wonder what became of the Ridgeway Ghost. Legend has it that he was last seen riding out of Ridgeway on the cow catcher of the *Cannonball,* a night train that used to run through town. It could be that he got toasted in the Ridgeway fire of 1910, which consumed a whole block. Although no funeral ever was held for him, he is *believed* to be dead. Even so, some strange things still happen around Ridgeway.

■ ■ ■

The Saturday Matinee

Marie Felzo

When I was growing up in Milwaukee in the early 1920s, ours was a family that had to count its pennies. But we were permitted one luxury that is among my most vivid childhood memories. Every other Saturday we went to a matinee at one of the vaudeville theatres downtown.

It was an occasion for all of us. I can see my tall father now, his face ruddy from a fresh shave, his mustache neatly trimmed, his blue work shirt exchanged for a white striped one with a stiff collar. Completing the picture of a "swell" was a derby hat and a velvet-collared Chesterfield coat. My mother, who had bustled about all morning in a nervous flurry to complete the household chores, was equally transformed. She had combed her fine black hair into a chignon and put on one of her "good" dresses — black crepe with beadwork — a black coat, and a broad-brimmed beaver hat stabbed with a hat pin. My sister and I, who were perhaps seven and nine when we were first permitted to accompany our parents, were dressed alike in grey corduroy coats, our Dutch bobs peeping out from beneath matching corduroy berets.

"Hurry girls!" Mother would call as we were getting ready. "And don't forget to take clean handkerchiefs." This reminder was a familiar one, but the hankies were necessary more often than not. Those Saturday matinees were never niggardly in providing entertainment. "The most thrilling acts this side of the Great White Way" were capped with a short play or a film that often was a tear-jerker, and the freshly ironed squares in our pockets would be reduced to sodden balls.

"Mother, did you lock the back door?" Father would ask, as we stood in the front entrance, ready to leave.

"Yes," Mother would call from the kitchen. She made sure that dish towels were neatly hung, chairs were pulled in at the table, and everything was left in good order. No unexpected visitor would find *her* house untidy.

My father would then inspect the contents of his billfold, carefully calculating how much he'd need for the afternoon. Satisfied, he'd tuck the wallet in his inside coat pocket. Then, taking a cigarette, he would fit it into a holder and strike a match on the sole of his shoe. As mother joined us, we would start down the street to wait at the corner for the streetcar.

"Where do you think we'll go?" I would ask my sister, as I tried to refrain from my usual skip and run and take a more ladylike pace.

"I don't know," she would answer. I could see she had a similar problem with her feet. "I hope we see Topsy and Little Eva." She was referring to a popular pair of singing comediennes, who did a burlesque of two characters from *Uncle Tom's Cabin.*

"I'd rather see Fanny Brice," I would reply. "I just love Baby Snooks."

"Me, too!" she'd say, quickly changing her mind.

Then we'd both giggle happily, envisioning the famous ruffled bloomers, enormous hair ribbon and huge candy sucker.

It was true, though. We did not know to which theatre we would go. That decision was always Father's. Sometimes he would have chosen in advance from attractions previously announced; sometimes he would study the newspaper on the long ride downtown, or he would look over the posters outside the theatre to help him decide.

Most of the theatres were on or in the vicinity of what was then Grand Avenue, and they had rather grandiose names — the Palace, the Majestic, the Alhambra. My childhood recollection of those theatres is one of opulent splendor: gilded furnishings, rich crimson carpets, great jardinieres, elegant mirrors and silken draperies. There were elaborately painted ceilings with goddesses strumming lyres or disporting themselves with coy cupids.

In the second balcony, where we sat, the accommodations were apt to be plainer. The stairways were steep and narrow and there was

61

no carpeting. As we waited for the show to begin, we sampled some chocolate nonpareils Father had allowed us to buy in the lobby. As the afternoon wore on, we would become so absorbed in the performance that we were oblivious to our moist and sticky hands.

The moments before the show began were full of such high anticipation that the sensation was almost painful. With the house lights on, the only thing visible on the stage was an asbestos curtain with ads for Sloan's Liniment, Smith Brothers Cough Drops, Palmolive Soap, and a variety of other products. Then slowly the lights dimmed and the asbestos curtain rose, revealing gold-fringed crimson velour curtains. Then these parted, and on the forestage, a circle of spotlight illuminated a placard on an easel announcing, "Blackstone, the Magician, and his stupenduous feats of legerdemain!"

Blackstone might be followed by a pair of hoofers, then some specialists in patter and pratfalls, a troupe of performing dogs, jugglers, monologuists, acrobats and dancers. My sister and I sat on the edge of our seats, our eyes shining with excitement as we watched such headliners as Edgar Bergen and Charlie, his brash dummy, Al Jolson and his blackface routines, W. C. Fields, Lou Holtz, Sophie Tucker and many others. Then when the spotlight went out and the acts were finished, there were still the feature movie, the cartoons, the travelogues, and the Pathe *News of the Day* to see.

By the time the curtain finally came down, we were emotionally spent. While waiting for the streetcar, Mother would sigh and say, "Alla Nazimova was wonderful, just wonderful," dabbing a stray tear from her eyes. Father, as he inserted another cigarette into the holder and struck a match against the lamppost, saved his comment for Will Rogers. "That cowboy has more sense than the President. 'All I know is what I read in the papers,' " he quoted, chuckling, calling to mind an image of the homely, gum-chewing philosopher spinning his lariat, and making wry remarks about the state of the world.

As for my sister and me, we boarded the streetcar in a trance, still living in a make-believe world. During the next week our play and games reflected the performances we had seen. By putting a piece of gum over my front teeth and making my voice crack, I could do a satisfactory impersonation of an old man a la Chic Sales. Or my sister, in a fringed shawl and our mother's high-heeled shoes, might whirl about the living room in her own rendition of a fiery Spanish dance.

As the days wore on into the second week since we had seen the matinee, little by little the prosaic world encroached upon our fantasies, and the vivid imagery of the most recent motion picture gradually grew duller and dimmer. By that time, however, we had already begun again to build our anticipation for the next show. We were never a rich family, but, through both good times and bad, one of the pleasures we could always count on was the Saturday matinee.

■■■

Women's Lib— Ashland Style

Catherine Whittier Lewis

W omen's Lib appeared at Ashland High more than fifty years ago, in the form of our "liberated" girls' basketball team, The Invincibles. We played the preliminary game, then the boys took over the court. We didn't feel slighted; it was just ladies first, though we were no ladies. The term tomboys would have fit us better, even though in our team pictures of 1918-1920 we are lined up, each with our right hand on the shoulder of the one in front and all of us looking demurely over our right shoulders! Once when an opponent told Laura Thibedeau, our star forward, whose long black braids flew out behind her as she zoomed across the floor, that she'd yank Laura's braids, Laura retorted, "You do and I'll rip your middy off!" And she probably would have.

Our modest uniform was a white poplin middy blouse with a colorful sailor's bow to brighten things up, and voluminous serge or satteen bloomers, plus long woolen stockings and white tennis shoes. "Happy" Gordon (whose christened name was a more sedate Adeline), Dorothy Hitter, Laura, Margaret MacDonald, and Letty Goeltz were among our star players. And of course there was Vivian Nelson, who wore a long dark skirt instead of bloomers, and spats over her slippers, and Isabelle Paton and Marie Coan. I don't know how I managed to stay on the team; perhaps it was because I never missed a practice. My Chicago & North Western Railroad pass, which allowed me to ride free to the cities where we played, probably didn't hurt either.

When we played games in Bessemer, Hurley, and Ironwood, we traveled by train and were overnight guests in the homes of the players of our host schools. Usually there was a school dance after the games. My prowess on the dance floor was less even than my skill on the basketball court, so I spent most of my time sitting along the wall, refining the art of "wall flower." Once though, in Bessemer, a fellow took me ice skating at an indoor rink. I *could* skate, and that glorious evening more than made up for many a night of decorating the sidelines at the dances.

Though we were "athletes" and liberated in our own minds, Ashland was not yet ready for girls in pool halls. So during our free time, while our brothers hung out at Hitter's Pool Hall, we girls usually made stright for our favorite ice-cream parlor. We walked the mile or two from school to the Palace of Sweets to gorge ourselves on wonderful, rich chocolate sundaes called googoos. We rationalized that because we walked, and because we were athletically involved in sports, we wouldn't gain any weight from the sundaes. Wrapped up as we were against the cold Ashland winter, it would have been impossible to tell if any one of us was overweight or not. We wore heavy coats, woolen middy blouses and pleated woolen skirts, and long johns (the only "double-knit" we'd ever heard of), high-topped leather boots, berets, and scarves wrapped round and round.

Johnny Paulos was our teen-age, 1920s version of Aristotle Onassis — Johnny's family owned the Palace of Sweets. Johnny always welcomed us warmly, especially if Dorothy were with us. He had a crush on her, so if he was on duty we were all assured of extra heavy dollops of hot fudge and peanuts on our googoos. Sometimes we were permitted to go in back to the kitchen where trays of freshly made peanut brittle, rich fondants and nougats were being prepared. Our idea of an evening out was not dining in a restaurant, but rather a trek to the Palace for googoos.

My family moved to Escanaba, Michigan, soon after I finished high school, and women's sports has certainly grown in the last few decades. But I still recall with fondness my first taste of Women's Lib, Ashland style.

■■■

Memories of a Country Preacher

Clay A. Schoenfeld

W hen my preacher father died in November 1950, I inherited his file of sermon scripts. In the upper left hand corner of each was recorded the date or dates on which it had been delivered, and where. In the upper right hand corner was an inscription — RWGF, or RWF, or R.

Until I discovered the code, the initials puzzled me. They turned out to be a self-designed Nielsen rating of sorts, standing for "Received With Great Favor," "Received With Favor," or simply "Received."

During more than 40 years devoted to serving small Congregational parishes in southern Wisconsin, the Rev. Albert Henry Schoenfeld was uniformly received with favor.

One former Lake Mills parishioner, Dion Henderson, Milwaukee bureau chief for the Associated Press, put it this way: "Saying A.H. Schoenfeld was a preacher is like saying Chartres is a church....He christened my daughters in the garden, and the consecration endured for years, so that the flowers turned their faces upward, and the weeds did not grow....I hope someday Clay tells how it is to grow up with a father who was a friend of God's."

My father was a very effective preacher for his time and place. His basic tenet was uncomplicated, an abstract of the Apostles' Creed: God created the world and sent His son to save it; whoever believes in Him shall have eternal life.

Besides those sermons, I have a scrapbook of newspaper clippings that A.H.S. kept from 1908 to 1948. They are a fascinating record, not only of the comings and goings of a country preacher, but of the whole flavor of a bygone era.

From the Dodgeville Sun-Republic, 1908:

"The afternoon service was conducted by Rev. A.H. Schoenfeld. His subject was 'Our Unnumbered Days,' and upon this topic he delivered one of the most scholarly and eloquent sermons ever listened to by any audience in this city."

The A.H.S. weekly message could border on the histrionic. I remember one Sunday when his new false teeth popped out during an especially vigorous moment, but A.H.S. fielded them in mid-air, popped them back in, and went on as if nothing had happened.

In a day before television, A.H.S. made high drama of The Word. His perennial Good Friday sermon was a classic. To the theme of "What do ye think of Christ?" A.H.S. would make a mock courtroom and take testimony from New Testament witnesses.

As he colorfully described first one and then another coming down the aisle to face Judge Schoenfeld, some members of the congregation actually would crane their necks for a glimpse of the approaching figures. They would include Pilate ("I can find no fault in this just man") to Thomas ("My Lord and my God").

Then A.H.S. would turn to the worshippers and say, "And what do *you* think of Christ? Mark well your answer!" It was enough to curl the hair on the back of your neck. Unsophisticated? Sure. Effective? You're darned right.

In many respects, A.H.S. was ahead of his time. Some scrapbook examples:

"In his Lincoln Day address, Rev. A.H. Schoenfeld dealt with conditions today relating to the emancipation of the Negro. The address was a plea for a square deal for the downtrodden, a strong protest against unjust and unequal conditions imposed by the dominant race in opposition to the development and uplifting of the Negro, a work but begun by their release from slavery by Lincoln." (Dodgeville Sun-Republic, 1912.)

"The laboring man is being better taken care of than the laboring woman. For a woman to labor is often considered a disgrace, but heaven help the woman who has nothing to do but dress up, paint on, and walk out. The working woman isn't getting a square deal." (Dodgeville Chronicle, 1914.)

From a farm and ranch background, A.H.S. drew agricultural figures of speech that meshed perfectly with the Old Testament and with his rural audiences. In southern Wisconsin in the 1920s it took no stretch of the imagination to see the Lord as your shepherd.

A favorite A.H.S. sermon was built around the text, "Except a seed fall into the ground and die it cannot bring forth fruit." The title was "In the Bin or in the Furrow?"

"How are you investing your own life?" A.H.S. would ask. "Are you like a seed of corn molding in a bin, or are you planting yourself in the soil of service?" No farmer in the audience could duck that question.

Because of his down-to-earth style, A.H.S. was in demand as a speaker on secular holidays as well as on church days. He had a Fourth of July bell ringer that made him a favorite at crossroads open-air picnics.

From the Dodgeville Chronicle, 1916:

"What is said to have been the largest crowd that ever assembled there attended the Latto Picnic on the Fourth of July. Just how many were present is of course not known, but the fact that 200 gallons of ice cream were sold before six o'clock is some indication.

"It is estimated that 2,000 people were standing to listen to the speaker. This was the fourth time that Rev. Schoenfeld has delivered the Independence Day address at Latto, and this was about the most effective oration heard in this part of the country for a long time."

But A.H.S. was more than a good preacher. He was a premier pastor. At least once a year he visited every family in the congregation — in winter those in town, and in summer the farmers.

I liked to ride along on those country jaunts, performing important chores: strapping and unstrapping the thong that kept the stick shift of our old Overland Six from jumping out of third gear, working the hand-crank windshield wiper when it rained, opening and closing the Can't Sag (Pat.Pend.) gates that in those days guarded every farm lane.

A.H.S.didn't spend time with just the well-to-do farmers who might increase their pledges. If anything, he sought out the less fortunate for special attention. Wherever he went he tried in some way to be useful.

One day in the palatial barn on the big Jewel farm we helped uncouple an aroused Belgian stallion from a screaming mare. Another time, we brought a large basket of canned goods to the hovel where — on the same bed — lay a frail woman nursing a baby with a head the size of a teacup, and a beagle bitch nursing a litter. For a little boy it was all a great primer in life's cross sections.

A clipping from the Wisconsin State Journal in 1928 imparts something of the flavor of the busy life of a country pastor:

"When Rev. Schoenfeld came to the pastorate of the Mineral Point Congregational Church 10 years ago, the church had 166 members. It now has 484. For local and benevolent church work, the congregation has spent $69,800 in the 10 years. During this period, Rev. Schoenfeld has baptized 307 people, performed 168 weddings, and conducted 367 funerals."

A.H.S. built up a wide acquaintanceship, so there were lots of calls to officiate at baptisms, weddings and funerals. In 1950 in Lake Mills he was still being summoned back to Iowa County to bury somebody he had baptized or married years before.

When I was young I never understood, much less appreciated, why somebody 100 miles away would summon my dad in the middle of the night to a burial. I guess I was jealous of the intrusion. With time I have come to know the urgency of the call.

A.H.S. was called because he knew people by name, and lived among them. And he did not limit his ministry to Congregationalists.

68

He was a friend to all who reached out, regardless of church affiliation of lack of it. That may seem routine now, but it was unusual in rural Wisconsin in the 1920s.

A.H.S. did have two sworn enemies: John Barleycorn, and any Democratic presidential candidate. Both were denounced from the pulpit regularly.

Interestingly enough, however, A.H.S. did not extrapolate his general global antipathies to the local level. The local bootleggers and moonshiners, and later the tavern keepers, all counted A.H.S. among their friends. And local Democrats were welcomed to the communion table side by side with God's own Republicans.

A.H.S. also had an affinity for blacks. The Rev. Jessie Smith from Tuskegee, Ala. made an annual guest appearance in my dad's pulpit and stayed overnight in the parsonage.

One year at the height of Ku Klux Klanism we were visited by three hooded figures who forced themselves into the house and backed my dad up against the parlor fireplace, a butcher knife at his throat.

"Reverend," one of them said, "you either goin' to stop importin' niggers, or else!"

My mother screamed. I cowered.

"Brother Taylor," my dad said quietly, "let us kneel and pray."

He had recognized the voice of one of his masked assailants. The Klansmen literally melted away. It was a magnificent demonstration of grace under pressure.

In his street attire and manner, A.H.S. was definitely a man of the cloth. But "out of uniform," he followed lay pursuits with verve and elan.

For one thing, he was an inveterate gardener, hand-cultivating big plots. Some years he raised chickens in a backyard pen. And we invariably butchered a live hog each fall.

After many years of gardening on somebody else's empty lot, my father finally put together a little farm of his own. It was 14 acres of so-so soil with a tiny house a mile or so off the north shore of Rock Lake at Lake Mills.

It wasn't much in the way of a ranch, but enough to allow my dad to put down his roots in his own land, and to rescue me forever from church-owned parsonages. Memories of that place sustained me in World War II foxholes.

The fame of A.H.S. as a gardener was wide. Even The Milwaukee Journal paid attention (1943):

"If the title of 'pastoral popcorn king' is ever conferred in the state of Wisconsin, it will go hands down to the Rev. A.H. Schoenfeld of Lake Mills. He has been preaching for nearly 40 years in southern Wisconsin, and wherever he has had his charge, there also has he had

69

a field of popcorn. This year the patch was large, because a lot of the popcorn was destined for overseas shipment to men in service.''

A.H.S. was a joiner. You name the service organization, and A.H.S. was in it. But over the years he reserved extra time and energy for the Masonry.

He also was a leader. For an obscure country preacher, he acquired a lot of regional, state and national recognition through his work in various organizations and in the offices he held.

Although he never missed a day of duty in the pulpit in 40 years, A.H.S. relished his month's vacation. Usually, he would teach at a Bible camp or substitute for another preacher somewhere, to finance a family excursion.

A cross country auto trip in the '20s was only a little less complicated than going to the moon in the '60s, but A.H.S. doted on the preparation, the navigation, and the new sights and sounds he later fed into sermons.

But my dad had an unworldly streak about him that I found aggravating. He simply refused to be concerned about tomorrow: ''The Lord will provide.''

After I got back from World War II, I tried to discuss retirement with him, but he saw no point in talking about the subject. The Lord would provide.

It was a couple of years later that I got an anonymous letter from a Lake Mills parishioner, pleading with me to persuade my father to resign voluntarily before dissident members of the congregation forced him out.

Before I could steel myself to go out to Lake Mills, I got a call from a friend there.

''Your father,'' he said, ''fell dead of a heart attack this morning while raking leaves on the lawn.''

The Lord had indeed provided.

■■■

Post Past

Jo and Jim Alderson

M ails arrived once a month, carried on a man's back," reported Elizabeth Therese Baird, speaking of the postal service at Green Bay in 1824. The first post office in what is now Wisconsin had been established in that city in 1821, but the government soon found it unprofitable to maintain mail routes to the community and outlawed further expenditures. Therefore, the letter carrier, a man named Bellaire, was paid partly by volunteer contributions by the citizens and partly by an allowance from the United States Quartermaster Department and the military post at Fort Howard. He and hardy carriers like him made the trip to Chicago on foot once a month during the winter. In summer, eagerly awaited messages were conveyed to the isolated settlement at irregular intervals by sailing vessels.

Before that time, messages for Wisconsin inhabitants had traveled with Indians and coureurs de bois. This kind of mail service may have been slightly more unreliable than today's, but at least it was free. Also free were the informal mail deliveries made by friends, relatives, passing traders, and circuit riders. The fishermen on Washington and Rock islands pressed their fish buyers into service as postmen. Even mail that started out through normal channels in the East had to finish its journey "however." A letter posted in Fairview, Pennsylvania, in 1823 is an example. The recipient, a Green Bay resident, had moved to Prairie du Chien before the letter arrived. How the message went from Green Bay across the state is unknown, but it reached its destination safely — only five months after it was mailed.

All in all, mail was delivered a remarkable share of the time, even when there was précious little address. About 1845 a marble statue was sent from France to Father Samuel Mazzuchelli, the renowned architect-priest of southwestern Wisconsin. Though the only address it bore was "M. Mazzuchelli, United States of America," it was delivered safely — a performance today's postal service would be hard pressed to repeat.

There was in the early days a strong correlation between the mails and the military posts. Settlers easily outstripped the post offices, but couriers between military posts filled in the gap by carrying regular mail along with official military dispatches. Frostbite was an ever-present foe of these military mailmen, and many were missing fingers and toes as badges of service. Frequently they had to sleep on the bare ground, which, no doubt, contributed to an arthritic old age. Snow blindness was also common. When the weather grew warm, their troubles were of a different nature; high water in swollen streams and rivers defied passage. Swamps and thickets were other pleasures of the trade; they could tear clothing and skin like knives. Under such conditions, keeping the mail dry was a problem. Oiled linen, deerskin, and bearskin were used for this purpose. In 1826 a penalty of twenty dollars was imposed on carriers for each time the mail was wet without such covering.

John H. Fonda was, for one trip in 1827, such a carrier between Fort Howard at Green Bay and Fort Dearborn at Chicago. His experiences are typical of the hazards these early postmen faced. Fonda wore a hunting shirt and leggings of smoke-tanned buckskin, moccasins of elk hide, and "a wolfskin *chapeau* with the animal's tail still attached." His "accoutrements of offence" included a mountaineer's rifle, a sheath knife, and two pistols. He carried his bullets in a mink pouch and his powder in a large horn.

Being "socially inclined," Fonda chose a Canadian named Boiseley as a companion for the trip. When the men were ready, Fonda presented himself to the quartermaster and was given a flat tin cannister covered with untanned deerskin. This box contained both military dispatches and letters of Green Bay residents.

"We left Green Bay on foot," he reported, "carrying our arms, blankets and provisions. We had to pass through a country, as then little known to white men, depending on our compass and the course of rivers to keep the right direction. . . . And as we continued to plunge deeper and deeper into the primeval forest, and to proceed farther on our course, the tracks of the fisher and mink became more frequent, and occasionally a wild cat would get its quietus in form of a rifle ball. Once, at night-fall, we encamped on a branch of what I now know to have been the Center River. This stream was a live spring, several yards in width; and was not frozen over. . . . Under a projecting branch Boiseley found the water perfectly alive with trout, and taking from his pack the light camp-kettle, he dipped out a mess of splendid speckled fellows. . . . In the evening, after collecting a huge pile of wood, we heaped the snow up to windward, and in the lee of the snowbank scattered some branches, on which we spread out blankets, and laid down with the packs beneath our heads, to listen to a serenade from the wolves.''

On the nineteenth day after leaving Green Bay, Fonda's narrative continued: "Grouse were to be seen budding on the trees, and we killed an abundance of them as we passed along. The grouse, with now and then a fish caught in the shallow rapids, formed our only food for several days. Until a little northwest of Chicago, we met with few Indians, all as hungry as ourselves. But joining a party of thirty Pottawattamies on their way to the Indian agency, we obtained from them a good meal of jerked venison and parched corn.''

When the pair arrived at Fort Dearborn, more than a month after setting out, they exchanged dispatches and returned to Green Bay by much the same route. "The Quarter-Master at Fort Howard expressed himself satisfied with my performance,'' wrote Fonda, "and he wanted me to make another trip; but as I had seen the country, which was all I cared for, I did not desire to repeat it. Getting my pay from the Department, and a liberal donation from the people, a portion of which I gave Boiseley, I left Uncle Sam's employ, and took up my old profession — a gentleman of leisure.''

Not until 1831 was a regular post office established in Chicago. Up until that time, the commandant at Fort Dearborn handled Chicago's mail. A man named Hogan became postmaster of the Windy City in 1832. He installed a private box system — a row of old boots, each bearing the name of a large receiver of mail, nailed to the wall. He also started a free delivery system, placing all unclaimed mail into his tall hat and setting out to finish the job in person.

In the same year, Pierre Bernard Grignon in Green Bay had the mail-carrying contract between his city and Chicago. He hired Alexis Clermont to make regular trips. Clermont went from Alexander Irvin's post office in Green Bay to Manitowoc, Two Rivers, Sheboygan, Milwaukee, and Skunk Grove and Gross Point, Illinois. It took Clermont and his Oneida Indian companion a month to make the round trip of four hundred eighty miles, and they were paid sixty to seventy dollars for conveying the sixty-pound pack. Clermont served on the Chicago route until 1836, when he was transferred to the Portage-Fort Winnebago route. While on this assignment, in 1839, he was the victim of snow blindness.

Along Lake Winnebago, another postman ran into trouble of a different sort. A man named Kevill carried mail between Winchester and Oshkosh, serving Butte des Morts and Brooks Road along the way. One day Kevill was ill and sent his son in his place. The young man had no trouble until he reached Brooks Road. The postmaster there was reluctant to trust so precious a thing as the United States mail to a fresh-faced boy unknown to him. After scrutinizing the lad, he inquired shrewdly, "Are you your father's son?" Upon being assured this was indeed the case, the proprietor handed over the packet, and the courier proceeded upon his appointed rounds.

Meanwhile, on the other side of the state, Judge James Duane Doty made application in 1823 to have Wisconsin's second post office established at Prairie du Chien, getting himself appointed postmaster in the bargain.

These Wisconsin mail routes were operating at a time when Los Angeles considered a year-old newspaper from the East "fresh." Everywhere in the growing country communication was a priceless commodity. Ever more speed was desired. Little by little the foot carrier gave way to the mounted rider, wagons drawn by oxen or horses, mail carts, sulkies, and stages. In addition to stage routes, Star Routes were set up to carry the mail from the dropping point to the people.

The post offices themselves remained rather casual, often being set up in general stores, where people naturally congregated. A young lady from Milwaukee visited Taycheedah in 1866 and wrote to a friend back home, "They have the most eccentric postoffice here, in a private house, letters are in a pantry, and I'm quite certain the man takes them out of a pitcher. I asked him yesterday if he had looked in all the cups, whereupon he went back and found another."

The first post office in Ephraim, in the 1860s, was even more compact. "It was confined to a small shelf, in one corner of Hans Jacobs' sitting room-kitchen-dining room-bedroom. On this shelf stood a tin box about a foot square and six inches deep. The box was the office itself, and was treated with profound respect by all, as being dedicated to the service of the U.S. Government. It was always kept carefully locked, and Mr. Jacobs would never permit anyone but himself to touch this sacred treasure chest. The contents of this box were rather disappointing. It had two compartments, in the smaller of which it held about a dollar's worth of stamps, also a pamphlet

74

of post office regulations. The larger compartment was for outgoing and incoming mail, but was usually vacant. The pioneers of Ephraim seldom wrote or received letters.''

Names of towns were of no little trouble in the early days. Kaukauna was known variously as Grand Cakalin, Grand Cackalin, and Grand Kakalin, among others. Some of this confusion may have resulted from illegible writing and illiterate writers, but even the inhabitants of a community could not always agree upon how the name should be spelled. Milwaukee was an example. Among the variants were Miliwaki, Milawakee, Milwaki, Milwalky, Milwakie, and Milwauk. Solomon Juneau, the first postmaster, preferred Milwaukie. Josiah A. Noonan, his successor, used Milwaukee. The matter took on political overtones, and the spelling varied with the party in power. It was difficult for mailmen to keep up with the politics of spelling.

Name changes further complicated matters. Brooklyn became Baraboo; Callamer became Merrimack and then Merrimac. Green Bay changed to Menominee on the same day Navarino changed to Green Bay. Many of these name changes were *not* voluntary. Postal authorities in Washington would not recognize towns with "landing" in the title; thus La Borde's Landing became Delhi. Officials also opposed names of more than one word with spaces or hyphens between, eliminating many early names of interest and beauty. One small post office had a peculiarly difficult time trying to find a name to suit Washington. The postmaster, T. A. Denny, reported, "I sent in different lists with five or six names on them, and they rejected them all...so finally I wrote to the Post Office Department and said, 'There's something peculiar going on here that you can't accept any of our names. How about Peculiar?' They wrote back and said, 'That will do!' "

Early post offices, like those of today, were not too profitable. One quarterly report shows that Delhi postmaster A. C. Steele earned ninety-nine cents and owed the government a balance of ninety-nine cents. A few quarters later, things were better. He earned $15.74 and owed only $14.16. Postal rates varied according to the distance the letter traveled in those days — three hundred miles being the cutoff between short-distance and long-distance mail.

Until 1847, when the first stamps were issued, payment of postage was noted on the envelope by the postmaster, either by manuscript markings or by hand stamps, which were carved out of wood, cork, rubber erasers, and even potatoes. The postmasters used all manner of designs: initials, shields, faces, grids, stars, targets. And even the issue of stamps did not subdue ingenuity completely. In April of 1851 the Mineral Point post office ran out of five-cent stamps with which to post letters going less than three hundred miles. So the ten-cent stamps were bisected diagonally, and halves were used on short-distance letters until a new supply of five-cent stamps was received.

Even in the early days, there were express companies operating in Wisconsin for those who did not wish to entrust their materials to the United States postal system. The express companies carried many things besides letters, but the regular mail had its share of unusual cargo too. One of the most notable was received at Watertown in 1856 — a small dog carefully tied up in a gunnysack and properly addressed to a well-known citizen. Commenting on the incident, a local editor considered it "no worse a perversion of the design of the postal system than the practice of some Congressmen of sending their washing home, under the mark of public documents and with their frank of postage free."

Wisconsin's mail stages generally visited a community once a week. The mails were eagerly awaited, and each resident knew when the stage was due in his locality. But to procrastinate is human, and more than one pioneer letter ends, "I would write more, but the stage is waiting for this letter." Though stage drivers were very accommodating gentlemen, the constant demand for more speed could not be met by horse-drawn vehicles. The job of carrying the mail began to shift to the railroads. Such service came to the largest cities in the late 1840s, much earlier than to small towns like Antigo, where a mail-and-passenger stage was operating almost up to World War I.

Railroads were fast and efficient, but they spelled the death of a more personal era when "junk mail" was unknown and every letter was a priceless event of interest to the whole community. And no train ever stood patiently puffing while a tardy patron finished penning his letter.

■■■

Sourdough Buckwheat Pancakes

Anastasia Furman

As kids on a Winnebago County dairy farm in the 1920s, we were sustained through the long winters by our sourdough buckwheat pancakes. Setting the sourdough batter was a process only Mother could put into motion, and we began pestering her for pancakes with the arrival of the first snowstorm.

"Soon's Father brings the buckwheat flour home from the mill I'll get them going," she'd say.

We knew the buckwheat was binned and waiting in the granary. Early in the fall old Tom Olson had threshed it with his steam-powered rig. When the main job on oats and rye was finished Father had persuaded him to mount his finest separator screens to thresh out a few loads of buckwheat. All that stood between us and our favorite breakfast was Father's sacking the buckwheat and taking it to be ground into flour at Schneider and Mader's gristmill in Winneconne.

About Thanksgiving time Mother set the sourdough yeast batter in a four-quart, straight-sided ironstone jar — the jar had to be large enough to prevent the batter from running over — and then she set the mixture on the reservoir of the wood-burning stove to keep it slightly warm so the yeast could grow. Next morning the batter was risen to the rim. Mother added a pinch of salt, a little syrup, and soda dissolved in hot water, and stirred the batter thoroughly.

The long, rectangular iron griddle had to be smoking hot, and greased with a chunk of pork fat speared, Paul Bunyan fashion, on a long-handled fork. A cupful of batter made three large cakes. I found these difficult to flip over, and learned that several dollops, eight or nine to the griddle, were easier to manage. But Mother never admitted that anything smaller than plate-size made a respectable pancake.

Whichever one of us was ready and waiting took over the pancake making while Mother fried salt pork, made coffee, and fed wood into the stove. When the cakes had browned on the underside and were bubbly on top we turned them. Mother maintained that water made a thinner, more tender cake than milk. She cautioned us to stir in more liquid if the batter began to thicken in the jar. "A buckwheat pancake," she said, "should stand as high as a silver dollar."

I put the first griddleful of cakes directly on my plate while my older brother took his turn at the stove. All of us liked our cakes hot, crispy on the edges, and covered with salt pork drippings and brown sugar.

By the time Father came to breakfast, he had already fed the stock, milked the Holsteins, and delivered the milk with team and sleigh to the cheese factory a mile down the road. Mother always sat down with him for one more cake, and old Shep would ease himself up to the table for his cake and the rinds from the pork.

Making our pancakes and eating them with strips of side pork and a glass of milk was part of getting ready for school, and the cakes stuck with us on our two-mile walk. Father had learned the substantiality of buckwheat cakes while he worked as a cookee in a lumber camp in the 1890s near Rhinelander. "I could roll out of my bunk and eat half a dozen. Nothing else held me quite so well until noon," he told us. Years later when my brother attended Ripon College, the first thing he learned was that the breakfasts served there would not stick to his ribs. He returned after the New Year loaded down with a sack of buckwheat flour and an ironstone jar of sourdough batter.

After breakfast what remained of the buckwheat batter was put away in the unheated pantry until night, when it was brought out again, renewed with buckwheat flour and water, and put to rise on the back of the range. This went on day after day until spring thaw. One morning Mother would surprise us at breakfast with a big crock of milk-gravy toast. We knew the buckwheat pancake season was finished.

Today a sack of buckwheat flour is almost as hard to find as a cook who knows how to set the sourdough buckwheat pancake starter.

Sourdough Buckwheat Pancakes

½ package dry yeast
½ c. lukewarm water
1 t. sugar
½ c. white flour
3 c. buckwheat flour
2 T. dark corn syrup
1 t. salt
½ t. baking soda
2-inch cube pork fat to grease griddle
3 c. lukewarm water

Mix first four ingredients; let stand several hours in warm place (80°). When light and bubbling stir in buckwheat flour and water. Allow mixture to stand overnight at room temperature, then add salt, syrup, and soda dissolved in hot water, and stir thoroughly. After a short rest the batter is ready for greased griddle.

Save a cupful of batter as starter for next morning's pancakes. Add flour and water each night and set aside to rise. The action of the yeast growing in the batter day after day gives the characteristic buckwheat flavor and texture. Discard the old batter and start out with new about every three or four weeks.

■■■

James Duane Doty:
Master of Chicane

Michael Goc

T he frontier era was a time when a man with the hungry gleam of acquisitive ambition in his eye had cast before him whole mountains of opportunity. Many a ninteenth-century American plumbed the untouched wilderness before him in search of the main chance. In pioneer Wisconsin, few men had an eye more vigilantly looking out for Number One than James Duane Doty. Federal judge, sneaking swindler; territorial governor, master of chicane; congressman, crook; founder of cities, briber of legislators — his contemporaries hung all these titles on Doty. Some of them fit his robust figure well; others are still open to the judgment of a new generation.

Like so many of history's lesser lights, James Duane Doty is largely forgotten today. He would have passed completely into the realm of footnoted obscurity already were it not for the unique monument he left behind. For James Duane Doty founded the city of Madison, named it, and — by means of some clever maneuvering — coaxed Wisconsin's first territorial legislature to make it the capital.

In October 1836, Wisconsin's original elected assembly met in the newly founded town of Belmont. Like so many frontier settlements, Belmont was more a state of mind than an actual fact. But in the eyes of territorial governor Henry Dodge, Belmont's two-story building — a rarity in Wisconsin at the time — and its handful of lodging houses for man and beast made a fine temporary capital city.

Henry Dodge — Colonel Henry Dodge of the Michigan militia — was a bluff soldier-politician, an original weaver of the cloth from which dime-novel heroes are melodramatically cut. He was a hero of the Black Hawk War, the commander of his own corps of dragoons, and the political leader of the populous lead-mining region of southwestern Wisconsin. He had been appointed governor of a territory that included all of present-day Wisconsin and parts of Iowa and Minnesota by President Andrew Jackson, a man known to be fond of borderland soldiers who also happened to be good Democrats. Ever the frontiersman, Dodge kept two horse pistols strapped to his belt as he presided over the legislature. Considering the volume of criticism aimed at him when he pronounced Belmont the capital, he probably

80

was glad they were there.

Dodge must have forgotten how much was at stake in designating even a temporary capital and how much more would be at stake when a permanent site was chosen. The value of the ground the rough-hewn solons trod would inflate overnight like moneybags in a speculator's dream. That a large city would spring up around the capitol building was the surest bet in the territory. Every boondocks schemer who could sketch a straight line chalked out a grid of streets in the wilderness, hoping his new town would become the favored site. And if the promise of future prosperity wasn't incentive enough, there was also an immediate grant of $20,000 from the Congress. Washington earmarked the money for improvements in the capital-city-to-be. Those funds would turn a dreamer's drawing into reality.

Still smarting from the criticism he had received because of naming Belmont the temporary capital, Dodge told the legislators he would support any site they chose for the permanent capital. At this news, land speculators all across Wisconsin rubbed their hands in anticipation. James Duane Doty led the pack. While the legislators wrangled over such weighty subjects as the face of the new territorial seal and whether larcenous Illinoisians had stolen what should be southern Wisconsin (thereby denying to the Badger State the dubious blessing of including Chicago within its boundaries), Doty laid his plans. He had already chosen the site he would promote for the capital. It was on the isthmus separating Fourth and Third Lakes, now called Mendota and Monona.

The Four Lakes region had long been recognized as speculatively promising. Much of the land was owned by absent easterners, including Michigan Governor Stevens Mason and fur-trade millionaire John Jacob Astor, both of whom employed Doty as their agent. As a broker for others, in his own right, and in various combinations thereof, Doty owned plenty of land in what is now Madison, Monona and Middleton, including portions of four sections over the common corner of which the capitol dome now rises.

In 1836, the only resident in the lakes area was a half-breed Winnebago who bore the aristocratic name of Michel St. Cyr. St. Cyr, his wife, and a small tribe of children lived in a twelve-foot log hut on the shore of Lake Mendota. An amiable fellow, St. Cyr extended humble if crowded hospitality to any traveler who happened by, including James Doty. Accompanied by St. Cyr and John Suydam, a Green Bay surveyor, Doty platted the new city. He called it Madison, after the former president who had recently died. He laid out a broad square in the center of town, ran streets out radially from it, and named them after the signers of the Declaration of Independence. To connect lakes Mendota and Monona, he penciled in "Wiskonsan" Avenue, using the spelling he insisted was the only correct one.

Now Doty's problem was to convince the legislature that Madison, a paper city far from vital water transportation routes and isolated from Wisconsin's two population centers in the southwest and the northeast — a city without buildings or people — should be named the home of state government. Challenges of this sort were not new to James Doty. He had arrived in Wisconsin in 1823, one of the first Yankees to settle here. The popular image of the struggling pioneer dressed in homespun, ax on shoulder and hungry family in tow, would not fit him. Doty had always been a pioneer in top hat and frock coat. He came to the state not in the least bit humble. At the ripe old age of twenty-three, he had been named judge of a court specially created to administer justice in the wilder portions of what was then western Michigan. Thus did Doty, a young man who had spent about four years eavesdropping in a Detroit lawyer's office, become the only judge between Lake Michigan and the Mississippi.

His "Additional Court," or "Doty's Court," as it came to be known, met every summer in Green Bay and Prairie du Chien. The vast area in between the two towns, much of which was still inhabited only by Indians, had little need of a judge or jury. But James Doty had a great need of it. For it was here he would make his fortune. He crisscrossed the wilderness on horseback, his eye on promising real estate. He envisioned cities, canals, railroads, and farms in country where not even Indians lived year round. In the course of his travels, Doty became the most widely known man on the northwestern frontier and the man who knew the most about the geography of Wisconsin. He dabbled here, invested there — a hundred acres on Lake Winnebago, a block of marsh in downtown Milwaukee, a few lots in Prairie du Chien. He struck up partnerships with prominent men like Astor, with whom Doty owned much of what is now the city of Green Bay.

In 1836, when he arrived at the new shrine of the possibly profitable now erected in Belmont, Doty found that no issue prompted more fervor than the selection of a new capital. Observed Governor Dodge: "Speculation and a thirst for gain appear to run into everything." Doty didn't like the wide-open atmosphere. In this, he was unlike the legislators, who welcomed all the attention and whatever else that came their way. And come it did — from Mineral Point and Platteville, bustling mining towns representing the most populous part of the state; from Green Bay, claiming rights of seniority as the oldest settlement in the territory; from Dubuque, whose boosters invited the legislators on the first junket, a party on the Mississippi bluffs. Fond du Lac was briefly a leading contender, which was fine with Doty, who owned most of it. Milwaukee and Racine were also briefly mentioned, but their remoteness from the already civilized sections of the territory made them weak contenders.

For a while, it seemed that Cassville would carry the day. The little city on the Mississippi offered the strongest of bids. Its leading citizen, Garrett Denniston, had erected a hotel — four stories high and of brick — to house the legislature. It was probably the only brick structure in the Northwest, and it was certainly the tallest. And if those bricks weren't impressive enough, Denniston sweetened his proposal with some icing the legislature would be hard pressed to resist. If the capitol were located at Cassville and Congress's $20,000 spent on improvements there, Denniston promised he would return the money to the legislature in two years, with interest. Thus Denniston and Cassville would give the territory a capital city.

But Denniston was no Doty. While the Cassville salesman boasted about brick and how he would return the legislature's money, Doty talked about available corner lots and how he could arrange their profitable return to the legislators themselves. Doty also contrived another way to smother the opposition. As the November nights grew cold and the green boards of the Belmont tavern that served as their dormitory shrank enough to let gusting winds chill the lawmakers' sleep, Doty produced a wagonload of warm buffalo robes. These he charitably distributed to the shivering legislators.

When the assembly emerged from beneath Doty's wraps and took up the capital question, an easy majority in the lower house backed Madison. In the thirteen-member upper house, the motion for the lake city scratched by, 7 - 6. However, motions to replace Madison with every other town on the list had to be defeated before the site was secured. Though the roll call of dashed civic hopes was long, Doty had it all wrapped up, and not just with buffalo robes. Sixteen cities were voted on and passed by. All were rejected 7 - 6 in favor of Doty's Madison. There was no joy in Cassville; the mighty brick hotel had struck out.

For weeks, Doty had worked around the clock, not so subtly pointing out the advantages and availability of Madison. Just *how* available was revealed later, when no fewer than sixteen legislators were found to be owners of property transferred by Doty in the paper city they had just named the capital. Some legislators were not honest enough to stay bought. Three of the sixteen accepted lots in Madison but didn't vote for it.

Doty had won the first hand, but the game wasn't over. Both Congress and Governor Dodge could veto any bill the legislators passed. Once again, Doty had his bets and his men covered. Wisconsin's delegate in Congress, George Jones, conveniently found himself the owner of some choice Madison real estate. He voiced no objection to the selection in Washington.

As for the Governor, Dodge was a man like any other, or so Doty thought. But when the champion lobbyist offered Dodge some lots in Madison, the Governor responded angrily. If he wanted land in the capital, he would buy it himself, Dodge retorted. Probably remembering those pistols Dodge was so fond of, Doty retreated, but not too far. Dodge's son Augustus accepted some lots in Madison. Dodge soon found himself hopelessly outmaneuvered. In a mournful letter to Congressman Jones, he lamented that everyone, including his own family, seemed to be caught up in Doty's scheme. In the end, the Governor let the cards lie where Doty had carefully placed them. Madison was the capital of Wisconsin.

The story should end with both Doty and his pocketbook swelling — one with pride, the other with pence. However, Doty's complicated finagling with the titles to his Madison properties snared him in a web of lawsuits for years. At one time, it wasn't clear if the deed he had given to the legislature for the capitol property was really his to donate. In addition, a year after Madison was chosen, the Panic of 1837 forced land values, especially speculative land values, to rock bottom. Doty found himself holding inflated pre-Depression mortgages he had to pay by selling land at greatly deflated prices.

Doty's loss wasn't total. Although he may not have made all the money he intended, his scheme was a success. His dream of a capitol dome crowning the isthmus between the two lakes had come true. The dome remains right where Doty — with a little legerdemain and a lot of buffalo robes — placed it a century and a half ago.

■ ■ ■

Up the Kickapoo With Miss Welch's Paddle

Jessie Eastman Holt

I f you began your schooling in Gay's Mills early in this century, I'm sure you will remember Miss Welch. She taught first and second grades for many years. She was tall and thin, and usually wore a black skirt, a white shirtwaist and a stern expression. She was a strict disciplinarian. If she couldn't pound knowledge into your head, there was always the other end. And for that she had a handy paddle.

In those days physical punishment was allowed for infraction of rules or lazy study habits. Not all teachers used this method, but Miss Welch's handmade white-birch paddle got quite a bit of action.

My turn for the paddle came during my second school year. That day started all wrong. There had been rain during the night, and as I started down the hill from home I slipped and skidded all the way down the muddy path on my seat.

Clambering back up the hill, I burst into the house to grab a pair of dry underwear, but was met with a roll of steam and the smell of Fels Naptha soap coming from the kitchen. Oh no! I knew the answer to my question before I even asked, "Ma, can I change my pants?

I slipped."

"No," she said, "everything is in the boiler."

Swiftly I shed the soiled garment, dashed out and down the hill, on the grassy side this time. I raced around "sugar-loaf" mound, past the flour mill and across the shaky wooden bridge over the Kickapoo River, and made the schoolyard just as the last bell started to ring. As I gained my seat, puffing heavily, Miss Welch gave me one of her foreboding looks.

At recess I sat against a tree with my mud-spotted dress wrapped around my legs. My classmates nagged me, "Aw, come on, Jessie, we need one more to play Red Rover."

"I don't feel like it . . . I think I'm coming down with something."

All day I walked very carefully, and when the last recess was over I thought I had it made. But late in the afternoon Miss Welch handed out slips of paper on which she had copied a riddle, and told us, "As soon as you guess the answer, write it on the paper, sign your name, and hand it in."

At four o'clock less then half the class had done so. The rest of us were told that we would have to stay until we did get the answer. So we sat, squirming, and staring at that piece of paper. Miss Welch sat at her desk, reading a book. Finally she rose and left the room. No one moved or spoke. Time passed. Then, like a gift from heaven, I had the answer! I was so excited that I jumped up and shouted, "It's a river! A river!" And just at that moment, Miss Welch came back into the room.

Across her bony knees, I had a good taste of that paddle. Worse than the whacks was the fact that when she turned up my dress, the other children had a good view of my nakedness. When she released me, I could see that Miss Welch's face was very red. I'm sure that I was red at both ends; I couldn't get out of there fast enough when class was dismissed.

Once at home, I didn't go into the house, but into the barn to visit my cats. I had long had a habit of bringing home stray cats, and now there were nine of them. I found several of them sleeping, picked them up, and sat, rocking back and forth. Pressing my face into their soft fur, I felt comforted. After a while I was calm enough to face the world again.

Of course the news of my troubles had reached home and I was greeted by a derisive chorus, "Jessie got a lickin'! Jessie got a lickin'!" Ma was putting bowls of some very good-smelling bean soup and a large plate of corn bread on the table, and said, "You kids hush now!"

The only one who hadn't teased me was my older sister, gentle Zella. When supper was over, she asked me, "Jessie, would you like to help me make some rock steps down the path?"

"I guess so," I mumbled. Then I got angry and yelled, "But first I want my pants!"

Ma smiled, and said, "Help yourself, they're still there in the basket."

I rummaged in the basket until I brought up a pair of homemade flour sack panties. On this pair the label was still readable: "Pillsbury's Best." I guessed that the flour sack hadn't been bleached long enough in the sun. I was just glad that it wasn't the pair that had the remainder of the advertisement: "Eventually, why not now?"

Zella and I armed ourselves with Pa's hoe and spade and attacked that miserable path. I think that I dug at it more fiercely than she did. When we were too tired to continue, we had made several steps, nice and level and skidproof.

* * * * *

Nowadays, hearing about the troubles in some of our schools, I wonder if Miss Welch's methods were not so much out of line. Nothing was made easy; we had to do our own thinking. We weren't given lessons with a choice of answers. I do know one thing for certain: When I passed into the longed-for haven of the third grade the lessons seemed easy. It is quite possible that I owe an apology to the memory of Miss Welch.

■ ■ ■

Winter Eggs

❖

LaVerne H. Benson

A round the time of World War I, supermarkets, as we know them today, and electric refrigerators in every home, were still a future event. I lived in Kenosha and many homes, ours among them, didn't even have an icebox. Our icebox in winter wass a shelf placed across the pantry window with the storm window open. In summer foods were kept in a dark corner of the cool basement. Perishable foods were kept in minimal supply; it was far safer to purchase them daily at the corner grocery store.

Like the proverbial ant putting away food for the winter, so did thrifty families. My dad planted a large garden every spring. The harvest of his garden was stored in the basement fruit cellar. The door to the fruit cellar was kept closed; it was dark and cool in there. In the fruit cellar were large wooden boxes filled with clean sand, and into these boxes went all the root produce grown in the garden — carrots, parsnips, rutabagas. Thus buried they kept fresh all winter long. The navy beans, along with the apples from our tree, which had been pared, cored, and sliced, were spread out on clean sheets in the attic to dry, then put in containers and placed on shelves which lined the walls of the fruit cellar. The shelves were also bulging with hundreds of jars of canned fruit, vegetables, and pickles. These jars were my mother's pride and joy, her badge of being a good, thrifty, capable housewife. The fact that they had cost her hours of backbreaking work to prepare and even more hours of standing over a hot wood-burning stove was insignificant. The pleasure she derived from gazing at the colorful array far outweighed any hard work entailed.

We children were usually sent down to the fruit cellar to retrieve whatever items mother needed to prepare meals, and we never really minded, except when sent for eggs. We had no chickens, unlike some of our neighbors, but mother had six brothers who were all farmers in the Green Bay area. Every year, late in the fall, either we would drive up to visit them or one of my uncles and family would drive down to Kenosha. We enjoyed the visits immensely, but the main purpose was to replenish our supply of eggs — at least three crates of them. Each crate held twenty-four dozen eggs.

Down in the fruit cellar my dad had two big twenty-gallon crocks. The eggs were placed in the crocks ever so carefully to avoid cracking, and covered with waterglass (a solution of sodium silicate and water which formed a colorless, sirupy liquid used as a preservative). The waterglass kept the eggs usable all winter long, though I remember towards spring my mother would wistfully mention she wished she had some truly fresh eggs for a change.

The temperature in the fruit cellar was about the same as the outdoors, so the liquid in the crocks got mighty cold as the winter wore on. Fetching eggs was our most dreaded chore. The only way to get them was to reach down into the frigid wetness of those huge crocks. The eggs of course being very fragile, had to be lifted out one by one. As the supply of eggs in the crocks dwindled, one had to plunge the bare arm deeper and deeper into the icy crock. The very properties of the waterglass that made it such a good preservative also lent to it a silky, slippery feel, which to us imaginative children was just plain slimy and utterly repulsive. It was something to be avoided if at all possible.

Though we were glad to have such a plentiful supply of fruits and vegetables during the winter, we felt we could have survived a few months without eggs. After all, we asked, "Who needs eggs in winter?"

■■■

Doctor Bertha

Judith Redline Coopey

A round the turn of the century it took an extraordinary woman to invade a traditionally male profession and to become something of a legend to those whose lives she touched. Such a woman was Bertha Reynolds, whose medical practice in and around Lone Rock and Avoca spanned the first half of the twentieth century. Her independence, strength, and determination fitted her for any challenge. It must never have occurred to her that women didn't do certain things. Bertha Reynolds *did* — whatever the situation called for, whatever her patients needed.

At one time there were nine doctors in her family, but she was the only woman among them. Though advised to become a nurse, Bertha would not be relegated to the traditional female profession. A doctor was what she wanted to be, and a doctor she became.

Bertha Elizabeth Reynolds was born in Thiensville on May 22, 1868, and raised among German settlers. School was conducted in German by a German professor. "You either spoke German or you kept your mouth shut!" Bertha recalled. She graduated at fourteen, taught in the country schools, and attended Lincoln Normal School when the family moved to Nebraska in 1892. But teaching was only a stop on the way to her lifetime calling. After studying chemistry and botany at the University of Nebraska, she graduated from the Women's Medical College of Chicago as an M.D. in 1901. She was thirty-three.

After a year as assistant physician for the new sanitarium in Prairie du Chien, Bertha went to Lone Rock and shared the medical practice of her brother, Nelson, until he left in 1904 to work in a Milwaukee hospital. With two doctors Reynolds in town, the people of Lone Rock distinguished between them by calling them Dr. Nelson and Dr. Bertha. The name stayed with her to the end of her days.

A small Wisconsin town's acceptance of a female doctor was not immediate in that era. She remembered one incident: "Soon after I arrived, the old doctor fell and broke a leg. When he was made comfortable, one of the bystanders offered to call me. 'Not her!' he said. 'Get someone who knows at least as much as I do.' "

Dr. Bertha never intended to be a general practitioner. "I was trained as an eye, ear, nose and throat specialist. But I received little cooperation from my patients. They absolutely refused to specialize in those ailments! I drifted accidentally into general medicine. First there were calls to go out on obstetrics cases. Then other emergency calls would come in. And there I was, a general practitioner. But I loved it, and would like to do it all over again."

For a country doctor in the early 1900s, getting to the patients was in itself sometimes quite an accomplishment. Dr. Bertha started out riding sidesaddle on horseback. Soon she was setting out on her rounds in a horse and buggy. In the winter, a horse-drawn cutter carried her through, although it was known to get stuck and even to turn over now and then. During the day, the doctor usually made her calls alone, but at night she often had a local man drive for her. One of these drivers commented, "For a mild-mannered woman, she's got the most stubbornness when there's a sick person to reach."

A narrow escape came one spring night when she and her driver had to cross the Wisconsin River to get to a patient in Avoca. It had been thawing, and the driver asked Dr. Bertha if she wanted to cross the bridge or drive over the ice. The ice was the shorter way, so she told him to cross it. As they proceeded, the horses seemed uneasy and kept edging toward the bank. At one point, they thought they heard the horses' hooves sloshing in water. They managed to get to the other side and spent the night at the patient's house. At dawn they returned to Lone Rock — by way of the bridge. The entire middle of the river had opened during the night.

Bertha loved spirited horses. One of her teams had to be hitched up inside the stable. Then the doctor would climb into the seat, take the reins, and nod to the liveryman to open the doors. Out they would tear like the very devil with Dr. Bertha holding on for her life. Dr. Bertha was never one to let the times pass her by, however, and she was the first peron in Lone Rock to buy a Model T Ford.

Eventually her practice ranged widely over the Wisconsin River valley. Acceptance grew into love as this gentle, efficient, dependable woman met challenge after challenge. "I've never taken out an appendix on a kitchen table because I'm not a surgeon, but I've sewed up many an accident wound on household tables, kitchen or otherwise," she said.

In May 1914, when a tornado killed four people in Lone Rock and injured many more, Dr. Bertha was on the job for forty hours. In the 1918 epidemic of influenza, she again worked tirelessly to treat the sick. Yet she was modest about such things. "Country doctors aren't heroes," she said. "People just get sick, call me, and I go to them."

She might have added, "any way I can get there," for getting there often was an adventure in itself. In the spring of 1923, Dr. Bertha received a call from Clyde, a small community south of the Wisconsin River. The Wisconsin was at flood stage, and it was impossible to cross by bridge or boat. Dr. Bertha heard that a young barnstorming pilot had landed at the Lone Rock airport, so she asked if he would fly her across the river. The pilot consented. As Dr. Bertha, at the age of fifty-five, climbed into the open cockpit, she asked, "What is your name, young man?"

"Charles Lindbergh," he replied.

"Well, Charles, I'm in a hurry. Let's be off."

They landed in a field near Clyde, and, as Lindbergh tinkered with his plane, the doctor treated her patient. Then they flew back across the river to Plain, where they landed in a school yard. The pilot, then only twenty-one years old and four years from world fame, gave rides to the students while Dr. Bertha made another call.

Someone once asked Dr. Bertha what aspect of medicine had changed most during her more than fifty years of practice. "Babies!" she answered emphatically. "In the old days, babies were born at home, and I would have to harness the horses and drive as much as twenty miles when one was expected. Sometimes I'd have to wait at the farmhouse a day or two before the baby arrived. I got ten dollars when it was all over, providing the farmer had ten dollars."

But her "babies" — she didn't know how many hundreds there were — were her pride and joy. In 1938 more than eighty of them showed up to help celebrate her seventieth birthday. Even today it is not difficult to find many of Dr. Bertha's babies in and around Lone Rock. "My patients were my friends, and I watched over their babies as if they were my children," she said.

In 1939 the University of Wisconsin presented her with a distinguished service award for her outstanding efforts on behalf of agriculture and rural living. There is another memorial to Dr. Bertha — a living one. It is a large pine forest east of the village along Highway 14. In the 1930s, when the government offered free trees to farmers for planting windbreaks, Dr. Bertha requested some for Lone Rock, "before the town blows away!" She encouraged farmers to plant as many trees as they could. Today, this formerly barren, abandoned land is a dense pine forest, thanks largely to Dr. Bertha's efforts. In 1951 the Sauk County Board established this land as the Bertha Reynolds Memorial Forest.

In 1940, at the age of seventy-two, Dr. Bertha sold her practice and drugstore in Lone Rock to H.A. Settlage and retired to Avoca. The retirement was temporary. With many physicians called into the service during World War II, doctors were scarce at home. So Bertha picked up her bag again and continued practicing until 1953.

It was easier to get around in the age of automobiles, but Dr. Bertha still was not without her narrow escapes. Once, while making a winter call at Pine Knob, her car skidded over an embankment and came to rest lodged against a tree. Afraid to get out, lest the fragile balance give way and the car tumble on down the embankment, Dr. Bertha blew the horn until someone heard her and came to the rescue.

Not a bookkeeper, she let her patients keep track of how much they owed her, and she often took her pay in produce or livestock or whatever the family could afford. One farmer paid his bill with a harpischord, which the doctor kept for many years. She didn't seem to mind if her patients couldn't pay, even though her own debts mounted up from time to time. Once she caught her nephew John preparing bills for those in arrears. She would not allow the invoices to be sent.

But her practice was rich with other rewards. Her patients honored her at a dinner commemorating her fifty years of service as a doctor. She received an engraved certificate from the Iowa County Medical Society. She got another from the State Medical Society of Wisconsin, plus membership in the society's "Fifty Year Club." At the Museum of Medical Progress at Prairie du Chien, her sidesaddle, medical bag, and instruments are displayed.

One of the sincerest tributes to this admirable woman came from the widow of her nephew Norris Kenny: "What can I add about Dr. Bertha? To me she was one of the most wonderful human beings that I have ever known — understanding, with a delightful sense of humor. Our many visits to her were a joy. She inspired devotion."

Dr. Bertha's long, selfless life ended on October 31, 1961. She was ninety-three. At her burial site in the historic Brown Church Cemetery in Bear Valley, an inscription reads, "She gave a life of service to this community." Dr. Bertha tended the sick and injured. She inspired those who knew her by her tireless example. She left a legacy of growing trees. And even now, sixteen years after her death, she is still giving to the community she loved. For when her name is mentioned, there is a stirring of pride, a smile warm with memories.

"Dr. Bertha? Oh, yes. I knew her well. She was a friend of mine."

■■■

Four-Jewel Movement

Lester P. Coonen

I n our very small town of Dundas, transportation was hardly taken for granted a half century ago. School and church were remote; both were in a neighboring town. There were twelve children in our family, and a variety of transportation challenges. In retrospect, each of our vehicles was, in its own way, a jewel.

We had a Dolson, the first auto in our town, but we didn't use it on Sundays because of its threat to our business. (My dad and my Uncle George had a general merchandise and farm implement store.) Buggy horses would be frightened and farmers were scornful of the puffing, smoking gadget. In fact, some buggy-riding farmers refused to share the road if they were approached from the rear. The Dolson was our weekday, business car, driven proudly by Uncle George.

For a long time Frank was our sole Sunday transportation. Frank was our horse, our oat-a-mobile. He endured up through my mid-teen years. Three gashes in the fur of his right flank told of his bronco heritage. That romantic ancestry, however, was not otherwise evident in his appearance. He looked old, decrepit and hangdog. Since he refused a checkrein, which would have forced his head high and proud, he drooped his loose-lipped black head and shaggy-maned neck very low, as though he were perpetually looking for whatever a horse might expect to find in the dust of a country road. A crack of the whip was good for only a half-minute acceleration, after which he resumed his lazy sleep-walking trot. A piece of paper on the roadside, however, momentarily whisked along by the wind, would startle him and transform him suddenly into a fiery western steed, dancing laterally, and snorting into high gear. But only very briefly.

Bales of hay went into Frank — energy of a sort — and garden fertilizer came out. He was important, and he seemed to know it. That made him at once our friend and our enemy. Several times, when we needed his hoof-power to take us to church, the barn door was found open and, instead of Frank, a blank. We would devise new guards for the stable door lock. It became a game of wits: horse against man. He would fit his aging teeth into or behind the mechanism of the lock, open it, and trot away. He wasn't mean or spiteful in this I think; just a lover of freedom, and grass.

We sold buggies, and whips and blankets and harnesses in our implement business. We should, therefore, have displayed the best of those wares in Frank's public life. We didn't. Our surrey was fancy enough, I suppose, but it was topless; just two seats with sky for cover, and disheveled Frank out front for power.

It was good fun, and festive, to squeeze into the surrey on a Sunday afternoon and head for one of our uncles' farms for visiting, fancy eating, and playing with cousins while the grownups played *Shafskopf.* Coming home at 10 or 11 o'clock at night was best of all. The peaceful clop-clop-clopping journey down narrow country roads had its charm. Little kids slept close to Ma in the rear seat while Pa talked of the Big Dipper and the North Star, and perhaps of the moon and the distant "sheet lightening," to the wakeful ones in the front. He'd make up little games such as watching the moonlight shadow of Frank as it slid along in the grass beside the road, short-legged or spindle-legged, according to the moon's elevation. "See the big dog in the grass," he would tease. Or he would sing softly the few lines he knew of "Twinkle, Twinkle, Little Star," or a few phrases of "The Grandfather Clock," drawing out especially long the ending, "and...the...old...man...died." No other sounds; but there were smells of horse (Frank-incense I suppose) and leather cushions and farm crops. Here was security and togetherness in our rural passage through an era.

Though we later acquired an Overland, the earlier car, the Dolson, was a real pride and exclusive joy to a kid like me. It was an adventure on wheels, simply because other kids couldn't match it. Its top was so high that, when the car arrived by railroad shipment from

Chicago, it was too tall for any of our several warehouse doorways. The top was summarily removed. There was no anxiety about tops, since we had been conditioned by the open surrey. It was not a quiet car: "You kids get out of the back yard," Ma would say, "I hear Uncle George coming." There was plenty of time to heed Ma's warning, for Uncle George was still about a quarter of a mile away.

That right-hand-drive machine had all the markings of Quality: four-cylinder motor; brass brake lever attached to the outside of the body; windshield. It had carbide lights that required four sequential steps to turn them on: 1) drop a few chunks of carbide into a water tank on the dash; 2) clamp down the lid so that gas pressure would build up as it was generated; 3) step out front to open each headlamp; and 4) strike a match to ignite the gas (which would arrive after about five minutes). The Dolson also had kerosene side lamps, to be enlisted in case of main-light failure. Much of what is now called pollution made for delicious smells — the carbide fumes, exhaust smoke, and leather upholstery. They were, in combination, most pleasant. The rubber tires, each held on by two cantankerous wheel-sized rings, were "guaranteed for 5,000 miles" — and *that* was a copy-writer's lie.

Car-driving was a mystery Pa never quite solved. When the business partnership was dissolved, and Uncle George left, Pa had to learn to drive. He managed; but a short trip with him was white-knuckled panic for his passengers. By then we were driving to church in our six-cylinder, seven-passenger Overland, with its shiny brass radiator and headlamps, and slanted leather straps to keep the top in an upright position. And there was a blue, six-inch-high policeman with wind-propelled arms on the radiator cap. The top was usually down in summer, folded so that it protruded rakishly as a kind of high, rear bumper. Pa "wore out" the top by backing it fitfully into neighbor Nieuhaus's wire fence; not once, but every time he drove the family to church. When we hit the fence, the car would quickly leap forward as if mightily tickled, then back again for one or two more noisy contacts. Pa worked the two foot pedals in alternate fashion, as though he were pedaling a bicycle. Not a blasphemous man, Pa issued a periodic "Oh pshaw." All the while, his passengers prayed quietly.

None of us, at the time, ever thought of our Overland or Dolson or surrey, or even Frank, as rare jewels, which they now seem surely to have been.

■ ■ ■

Swinging Was Our Thing

❖

Norma E. Erickson

When I was a child, fifty-odd years ago, we had a sure-fire way to solve the problems of a long hot summer. Part of the architecture for most homes in those days was a big porch, open or screened in. And practically every family with a boy in high-school manual arts class had a porch swing.

My brother Hal made our swing. And my father hung it from the porch ceiling on long chains. It made a harsh "kre-ek-krunk" sound as we swung back and forth. "Roy, you must oil the porch swing hooks," Mother would say. Numerous oilings did little toward quieting the noise of our swinging.

The end of the porch where the swing was hung was covered, spring through fall, with a lovely green clematis vine that shared its purple blooms with us all summer. It also insured us a certain amount of privacy and protection from both the splattering of rain and the glances of passersby. At the same time, though, you could see through the leaves, keeping track of what was going on along the street. That swing with its attendant porch became our summer living room, children's play room, and lover's retreat.

My mother often sat there in the cool of the morning, shelling peas or snapping beans for dinner. Sometimes I sat with her, my feet curled under me. While she kept the swing in gentle motion with an occasional push, we would talk.

"What did you play when you were a little girl, Mama?" I loved to hear the stories about her childhood.

"Oh, I played with my clothespin dolls. I made them morning glory hats and sent them off to church and school."

A rainy day would find me in possession of old "Kreek-Krunk." Sometimes I was content to curl up with a book. Other times I'd stand up and, holding tightly to the chain, I'd pump the swing crosswise of the porch. In my imagination I was the engineer, brakeman, and conductor of a train rushing through the countryside. Then I'd hiss and brake my swing locomotive as I stopped to pick up passengers. Often my passengers were real — neighbor kids who came to play with me.

"Aw, come on, let us on!"

"B-o-a-'-d for Mineola, Albuquerque and Ches-a-peake Bay!" I would chant. My geography wasn't too accurate, but the names had a nice rhythm. That porch swing train could travel anywhere we wanted to go.

There were times when my older sister and her girl friends won the swing by demanding, "Mo-ther! Make this child go away. We're having a private discussion." The porch was off limits when they had "secrets" to talk about. But nothing was said about *underneath* the porch being taboo, so I would crawl through the lattice covering the open end of the porch and sit there listening to those silly girls. All they talked about anyhow was how handsome some boy was, or what new clothes they could coax from their folks, or whether their mothers would let them do their hair up.

When my brother and his friends sat there, their conversations were mostly about "advancing the spark" on Hal's Dodge roadster. Or they talked about getting summer jobs in the Forestry Reserve and making a lot of money.

My mother and father and I often sat in the swing in the evenings after supper. Their voices were a quiet hum accompanying my flights of imagination. Sometimes these were interrupted when mother invited a neighbor, out for an evening stroll, to join us on the porch for lemonade and cookies — and a little gossip.

"Why don't you go play in the yard for awhile? You can count lightening bug flashes," Mother would suggest, giving me the "little pitchers have big ears" treatment.

The summer my sister got engaged the swing must have heard the plans she and her young man made for their future together. After a Sunday afternoon trying to convince them that Elsie was too young to get married, my mother sat between them in the swing and agreed to give them her blessing. They spent a lot of their engagement time sitting in the swing. When mother thought her future son-in-law and Elsie had been holding hands and swinging long enough, she would shake the dust mop out of the upstairs hall window. A shower of dust drifting down from the porch roof gave the lovers the hint to say goodnight.

I guess the time I enjoyed swinging the most was after supper on warm summer evenings. The high spot for me came just at dusk, when the first evening star came out. That was when my own concert began. Mother's alto and Elsie's soprano blended on the old ballads. *My Old Kentucky Home,* and *Flow Gently Sweet Afton* were some of my favorites.

Our hymn time always included *The Old Rugged Cross* and *Nearer My God To Thee.* Then my sister sang the last number of the concert.

After all these years, I can still remember the words to *The Man In The Moon Who Sailed The Sky.* We would swing a little longer. Then it was time for me to go to bed.

■■■

A Bout with Dame Fashion

Fred L. Holmes

O
ne of the unmentionables of a bygone generation's daily life was the woman's corset. Boned, stayed, and tightly laced, it was for many decades an indispensable article of apparel for milady who bowed to fashion's decrees. Men, too, countenanced the fad, but only — asserted the anti-lacing crusaders — because they didn't have to wear them. "Let man try for himself," wrote one of them at the turn of the century, "what it means to spend a day in well-laced corsets, a summer's day preferably, when the blood-vessels respond to the dilating warmth. It would serve him for a liberal education and temper forever his strange masculine and inartistic enthusiasm for wasp-waists. For it would prove to him once and for all time the cost at which the nineteen inches are gained."

Wisconsin had its role both in the development of these "instruments of torture" and in their ultimate disappearance from the scene of Vanity Fair. Among the corset designers of the nineteenth century was the now-forgotten Freeman L. Tripp, an inventor and the owner of a women's apparel shop in Eau Claire early in the sixties. In later life he cited as his most noteworthy achievement the hat fastener he had invented to eliminate the need for ribbons tied under the chin. Fifteen years earlier, in 1863, he had patented another article in which, one hopes, he took less pride. This was a corset fashioned with whalebone, which was already in general use as stiffening for the hoop skirt. This invention he sold to a traveling salesman from Chicago for five hundred dollars. A few years later he devised another model, a long-waisted garment which he sold for the same amount. Among his other creations were a lowbusted corset emphasizing the wasp waist, which immediately became popular, and an abdominal model that proved to be a money-maker.

Well into the twentieth century women continued to lace themselves tightly into heavily boned garments to achieve the minimum waistline, eighteen or nineteen inches being the goal. Surely none but Dame Fashion could have imposed so rigorous a discipline! "That the stays are indeed tight," protested Dr. Arabella Kenealy in 1904 in the *Nineteenth Century* magazine, "is shown by the fact that although the physique and internal organs expand in every other direction, the waist of adult woman *is actually less than that of the girl between ten and twelve."*

The wearing of corsets was of course by no means new in history; for centuries it had been fashionable among the leisure classes of Europe. But it was not until the late nineteenth century that the working classes adopted the practice. "At the present moment," Dr. Kenealy wrote despairingly, "the use of corsets is more universal than has hitherto been known. . . .It permeates the humblest levels of society. You shall not find a housemaid or kitchenmaid, a shop-girl or a little slave of all work, who does not pinch her waist to a morbid and ridiculous extent. The thing has become, indeed, a national evil." Nor did she dare hope that reform could be accomplished within a generation. "Progress is far too slow a thing for that."

But the next generation did see the doom of tight lacing, thanks to the fulminations of the medical profession, the mania for reform which seized the early twentieth century, and the growing emancipation of women on every front. The injuries caused by tight lacing were described in detail by scientists; one of them even performed experiments with corseted monkeys, the results of which were "as disastrous as they were instructive." And Dr. Kenealy was not the only woman to appeal to feminists with the warning that "so long as one sex wantonly curtails its powers and the other one does not, so long will the sex that does be heavily and insuperably handicapped."

At about the same time the anti-lacing issue was introduced into the Wisconsin legislature. In January, 1899, a resolution "relating to the health of old maids" was introduced by Assemblyman Henry L. Daggett, a farmer member from Bear Creek in Outagamie County. It was not printed in the *Journal,* but from newspaper accounts it would appear that it called for a joint committee to draft a bill prohibiting tight lacing. It was referred to by reporters as Daggett's "anti-lacing resolution."

Most of the newspapers quipped about the matter, treating it as one of those "diversions that serve to brighten the monotony of routine of charter-tinkering and Bear Creek bridging." According to the Eau Claire *Daily Telegram,* "the resolution was introduced as a joke and the assemblymen are having all the fun out of it possible." That Daggett's fellow legislators did so regard it tends to be substantiated by the scanty record preserved in the *Assembly Journal.* There, in two brief entries, it is stated that Resolution 11A, "relating to the health of old maids," was referred successively to the Committee on Public Health and Sanitation, the Committee on Agriculture, and the Committee on Public Improvements! Of its final disposition no mention is made, nor is it included in the numerical list of resolutions appended to the published proceedings.

Yet I have been solemnly assured by several members of the 1899 legislature who are still living that the stout, chin-whiskered Daggett was entirely serious in his proposal, as were a considerable number of his colleagues. One may not assume, moreover, that he merely voiced the prejudices of his unsophisticated rural constituency. He was a man of some education and business experience. After acquiring a business college training, he had managed retail and wholesale stores for some years and had been the foreman of a freight depot at Fond du Lac before moving to Outagamie County in 1881 to start a dairy farm.

All the contemporary evidence suggests that Daggett was quite serious, and one suspects that he failed to appreciate the humor and jocularity his proposal evoked in the press. At a committee hearing where it was demonstrated that a woman could not speak above a whisper when encased in one of the corset contraptions of the day, Assemblyman Daggett shouted, "I don't wish to offend the ladies. But the evil is worse than the binding of the feet of Chinese women."

Throughout the session Daggett enjoyed the dubious prestige of widespread unpopularity and ridicule. A group of Watertown women presented him with a huge floral corset, tightly laced. The dance program for the legislative ball held on April 20, which was designed by Assemblyman Louie A. Lange, editor of the Fond du Lac *Daily Reporter,* showed Daggett as a knight with sword in hand about to launch an attack upon a monster corset, realistically drawn. At the bottom were two lines from Shakespeare (credited to Assemblyman Chris Sarau!); "Lay on, McDuff; and damned be him that first cries 'Hold, enough!' " Weeks before this, at the time of the legislative reception in late February, the press reported that Dagget's wife had become "so incensed at his notoriety that she refused to come to Madison to attend the reception."

At the close of the session the disillusioned Mr. Daggett returned to his home. But the lampooners were not yet done. On May 4 appeared the following item in the *New London Press:*

"This week Hon. Corset Daggett's plunder-box arrived at Bear Creek...a chest made in Madison for the legislators to store and carry home their stock of stationery, pencils, Blue books and other legislature papers. Daggett's was decorated upon the outside by pictures of handsome women in their nether garments, with waist enclosed in a certain brand of corsets. It attracted more attention at the Bear Creek station than a circus. There was a long string of people going to and from the depot to view the curiosity yesterday."

Serious-minded people used the episode as a point of departure for more sober reflections on the evil that Daggett sought to eradicate.

102

One of them was the brilliant Amos P. Wilder, editor of the *Wisconsin State Journal,* whose son Thornton was later to achieve literary fame. While Daggett's resolution was still before the legislature Wilder wrote editorially that while the resolution itself was presumably not to be taken seriously, "it may not be amiss to say that the corset habit is on the decline. Especially in the cities where well-informed club and college-trained women to a great extent set the fashions, has the wasp-like waist gone glimmering among the things that were. In the rural districts misinformed young women still cramp and deform themselves into an abnormal, unhealthy and revolting parody on the beauty of the human form divine, unmindful of the official measurements of the faultless Venus de Milo (26 inches, if memory serves us right); and in the city, too, young women, especially of the sensational walks of life and those whose thought is too largely on appearances and not on the earnestness of an earthly mission, walk the streets with an attempt at neatness of form which misses the mark to all intelligent observers."

The medical profession, asserted Dr. Wilder, was united in its opposition to "the abhorrent practice." The "penalty paid in the experiences of motherhood is a terrific warning." Anyone who minimized that penalty had but to consult the books on the subject.

"But love of admiration," he conceded, "is the most powerful motive that controls the minds of a considerable portion of the weaker sex; and the most effective way of driving the corset into the limbo where the hoop-skirt and the slashed skirt continually do cry, is to convince women that there is nothing attractive or winning in any waist that is not anatomically correct.

"Mr. Daggett should beg leave to withdraw his bill, and substitute a resolution to the effect that no single man of the legislature is willing to entrust his hopes of connubial bliss to any home dominated by a woman who distorts her loveliness by artificial contrivances. As for the married men of the legislature, nothing they can say or do cuts any figure."

Mr. Daggett did not withdraw his resolution, but it was effectively smothered by the ridicule of colleagues and newsmen and the hostility of the women who resented being told by any man what they could or could not wear. Nor did he have another opportunity to carry on the crusade. Mr. Daggett was not among those present at the next session of the legislature.

■■■

Pearl Diver

Mel Ellis

I am always going back to see if the big, black clams still cluster along the clay bottoms of the winding Rock River, hoping to find one with a pearl luminous as the moon. It is an unfinished piece of business which has been smoldering like gold fever since the day, as a sun-dried crisp of a boy, my questing thumb felt through a mess of clam meat and juice, touched the first hard nubbin of pearl, and turned it to the light where it flashed pale pink and white and light blue in the blazing sun. I held the seed pearl in the palm of my callused hand, and my fingers, with their ragged nails, trembled so much the pearl quivered with opalescent light. Then and there, any plans my mother had for making me into a concert violinist drained like rain off a hill to become one with my mysterious river.

The idea that my beautiful and bountiful river could hold such riches as might tempt grown men came late in life. I was already ten, and though I knew where the terns and coots nested, what sloughs to spear carp in, what bays held the largest northerns, which gravel bars the walleyes came to after dark, I had never dreamed that somewhere along that coppery river might rest a clam with a pearl

104

big as a pigeon's egg and brilliant as the flame of the candle which each night lighted the way to my cot on the porch.

Subsequently I found many pearls. Never the perfect pearl, but rare beauties nevertheless — some pink, some white, and a few as black and shiny as a drip of tar. But in the miraculous instant that I brought that first tiny pearl out of obscurity, I was caught up and consumed by the promise of such riches as all prospectors must dream about. I became feverish with such anticipation that the catching of ten-pound fish was relegated to the realm of triviality. Looking back now, I can well understand and appreciate the visions that must have compelled prospectors to die crossing desert and mountain in quest of treasure.

Fifty years ago, clamming along the Mississippi and other midwestern rivers was still a thriving business because synthetics hadn't yet replaced the pearl button. Itinerant wraiths of women in gingham and overalled men roamed hopefully and unobtrusively from river to river, searching for the big one, but settling mainly for seed pearls which were sold for ornamenting other jewelry. They earned just about enough to keep them in bread and whiskey. And though they never quite reached it, they were trying for the rainbow.

In the beginning, I knew nothing of pearls, nothing of the men who hunted them. Then one night, having gone to my cot, I lay listening for the splash of fish on the river, the inquiry of a night heron looking to camp, the whimper of the little owls in the oaks. I heard them all, and also a mallard quacking in alarm. Then came a strange sound, and lifting to an elbow so I could look through the screen, I saw flashlight beams crisscrossing the glade.

Next morning there was a tent, and I discovered that one woman and two men had moved in during the night, though for what — since they had no fish poles — I couldn't imagine. When they began bringing boatloads of big, black clams to shore, when they sat cross-legged opening them, discarding the shell and flesh, I was mystified. But having, like a young brush buck, an aversion to coming too close to strangers, I stayed my distance and waited until that night to ask my father what they might be doing.

"Likely looking for pearls," he said.

Pearls! In my Rock River! Right here in the black clams which were so plentiful that walking over a bed of them was like walking across a field of stones.

I didn't sleep much that night. The next morning I threaded my duck skiff along their trail, careful to stay a respectable distance, and when they began collecting clams I put out some cane poles — with no bait on the hooks — so they wouldn't know I was spying. The men, without removing any of their clothes, waded chest deep in the river, feeling for the clams with their feet and dunking at intervals to bring them up. When they had a boat loaded, they rowed to the nearest shore and began to open them and search for pearls.

I wrapped and stowed my poles and hastened around a bend so I'd be out of sight. Then I began collecting clams. When I had a black mound of them in the stern of the little skiff, I paddled back to the cottage, got a knife, and sat down to open them. But it wasn't that easy. The harder I tried, the tighter the clams closed their shells. I tried smashing them between two rocks. They broke open, but the flesh was crushed and juice spattered on my bare legs. I scraped and bruised and cut my fingers, but I found no pearls.

It had been obvious that the men had no difficulty in opening the clams, so I bided my time, and when they were once again hunched over a mound of black shells, I crept through the grass to where I could watch. It was instantly clear that the knives they were using were thrust to a point just above the hinge and then rocked back and forth. I backed carefully away and then went back to my own pile of clams. I made a few false passes with the knife, but when I hit the muscle, the clam relaxed and I could pry the shells apart. Then I went carefully through the meat, and though I found a few pearls, they were encrusted in the shell and irretrievable.

I remember as though it were yesterday when I finished with the last clam. The sun was boiling down out of a brassy sky. A cloud of flies had descended on the clams and me. My fingers were crisscrossed with cuts. The clam juice was congealing on my body in uncomfortable and alien scabs. In the end, it was the flies rather than an overwhelming desire to find pearls which drove me back into the river to get another load of clams.

I went through the whole painful procedure again, but found no pearls. I think that might have ended it, but the next day when I walked into Juneau to deliver bullheads to the Northwestern Hotel, the bartender showed me three seed pearls which he had taken in payment for some moonshine. I knew at once they had come from the professional pearlers camped beneath my porch.

He let me hold the pearls, and though they were neither large nor perfectly round, they were beautiful. One was snow-white, another was pink as a sunset, and the third was black and shiny as a speck of coal. I completed my bullhead deliveries on the run so I could get back to my skiff for another try at pearling.

I don't remember exactly, but I think I went for three days without finding a pearl. Then one day when the men were out on the river, I found enough courage to approach the woman who stayed in the camp and did the cooking. She looked terribly old, though I don't suppose she was more than forty. She was fat and wore a man's shoes without

106

any socks inside, and though I didn't get close, I could smell moonshine. Her hair came down from a bun on her head in ragged strands like horsehair from an oriole nest which has been in the wind so long it has started unraveling. She was sitting on a stump drinking coffee from a tin cup when I came up, and for a while she just looked at me. I was about to turn and run when she said, "Yes, Boy?"

It was a strangely wonderful voice, deep and throaty. It stopped me in my tracks. Although she had spoken but two words, it came to me at once that she was lonely and beaten and sad. I stared a long time before I realized I was staring. Then, to cover up, I said, "Could I ask you some questions?"

She laughed a little, and the sound of her laughter was as soothing as the sound of her voice. She replied, "Well, I guess so, because I don't have to answer them if I don't want to."

I looked down at my feet. I don't suppose I looked up at her once while I was talking. Perhaps sensing that I was frightened, she told me to sit down, and asked if I'd like some coffee. I took the coffee. It was so bitter I could hardly swallow it, but I made a pretense of drinking. After a while she asked, "What do you want to know?"

So, still looking at my feet, I explained that I wanted to learn how to find pearls, that I knew about getting the shells open, but that I didn't know how to go through the clam meat without dumping it into a pail and fingering through it.

She got up and went to a pile of empty clamshells. A cyclone of flies lifted as she bent over to get one. Then she came back to the stump and told me to watch while she ran her thumbs along each side of the shell under the meat to the spots where the pearls — if there were any — usually lay. In a low, hoarse voice that was almost a whisper, she explained that you had to feel the pearls rather than see them, and that it was even good to shut your eyes while thumbing along beneath the meat so as to be able to concentrate on the sense of touch.

"When you feel one you'll know it," she said. "Then get it between your thumb and forefinger and put it up under your upper lip where it'll be safe. Then when you've sucked it clean, spit it into a small bottle."

Then she was silent. After a time, I dared to look into her face and ask, "Is that all there's to it?"

She gave her tin cup a toss and coffee grounds went spraying into a clump of cattails. She looked into the bottom of the cup as though there might be a pearl in it, and then she said, "That's all. That's all that you'd understand." She got up heavily and sighed.

"Thank you," I said, turning away.

Out of the corner of my eye I saw her turn toward me again, so

107

I waited. She put a hand to her face and then said quietly, "Don't thank me, Boy. It's no life, believe me. Forget the pearls. You'll starve trying."

I doubt that I understood at the time what she was trying to say to me, but I waited until she went into the tent. Then I walked as far as it was necessary for politeness before breaking into a gallop.

It wasn't until the next day that I felt the first nubbin beneath my thumb and brought the first seed pearl to the light of day. It was almost as big as a perch's eye, and though not completely round, it had such color as took my breath away. I quickly put it into my mouth, sucked it clean, and then, holding a small medicine bottle to my lips, spit the pearl into it. It shone like captured sunshine, and I just had to sit and marvel at it though every fiber of my being was for getting on with my search for greater riches. I found two smaller ones that day. Even my family was excited by my discovery. We sat around the kerosene lamp until way past my bedtime admiring and talking about the pearls.

After that, there was no time for anything else. My bullhead customers began to complain; Buck, my dog, had a droopy, sad look in his eye because I had no time to hunt and swim with him; my brothers and sisters took to whispering about me; and the fishermen who saw me armpit deep on a bed, feeling for clams with my feet, asked what that crazy kid was up to. I grew lean as a heron. My skin got a leathery look. There were circles under my eyes because I got up so early and was still opening clams long after the mosquitoes had claimed the night as their own.

But when I got back into shoes to go to school, I had a small wine glass full of some of the most beautiful pearls a man could ever want to see. I used to spread them on a card table and sit by the hour while the light, like the notes of a song, played a hundred variations on the same theme. None of the pearls was round enough to be worth much money. I knew that, but it made no difference because I didn't want to sell them anyway. When my father suggested I take them to the jeweler to see how much I could get for them, I always found some excuse for putting it off.

Then came the day when I went next door to show the pearls to my grandmother's new boarder. I had spread them on the card table, when Buck came running through the room and upset the table. All the pearls went down the large, circular, hot-air register of my grandmother's furnace.

I nearly died. And sometimes I think a tiny part of me did. I braved the searing heat and went through the dust and grime which had been accumulating in the old furnace for years, but I never found one of my precious pearls. I figured I had wasted my entire summer, but now that I look back, I know that the summer wasn't wasted.

Now I know that the real value was not in the pearls but in the dream. I have never dreamed so grandly since, and in all the years between, I have never come to any adventure with such a singleness of purpose. And in losing the pearls, I learned the hardest lesson: All life is transilient. Only the dreams endure.

■■■

The Old Mill

Arline Ensenbach

N ext to Cedar Creek on Columbia Street in Cedarburg stands an old mill, proudly defying time and weather. Young people hurry by, scarcely noticing it, but oldsters regard it as a treasured landmark. The mill, five stories high and more than 125 years old, has stood solid while generation after generation has passed by, wearing hoop skirts to bikinis, Civil War apparel to Vietnam uniforms. My grandfather, Burghard Weber, built this mill in 1855, a formidable task completed without benefit of electricity or modern equipment.

Grandfather came from Germany in 1855. A wooden mill on the site had burned down the year before and the owner of the property, Frederick Hilgen, hired Grandfather, a stonemason contractor, to replace it with "a sturdy stone mill, one that will last a century." Hilgen wanted a tall building that would tower over the village. Grandpa, only 21 years old, was delighted with the challenge the big project offered. He mulled over his plans for weeks, searched the area for the best limestone, and hired a number of strong, brawny-armed young men to help him. Handling those heavy stones required workmen with sturdy backs and arms.

His research indicated that the best limestone was in the bed of Cedar Creek, at the building site. To get at it he diverted the creek easterly. Quarrying right at the construction site also eliminated tedious, time-consuming cross-country hauling with horse and wagon. The quarried stone was formed into large blocks, and the foundation and first story were laid, fused together with buff-colored mortar. The walls at this point were three feet thick, eventually tapering to a width of 30 inches at the top of the building. It was early spring when the work started, and it progressed steadily. With the start of the second story, a small ramp was built and wheelbarrows were used to haul the heavy stones up the incline.

In 1856 the ramp was raised still higher to accommodate the blocks and oak beams to build the third story. For the fourth and fifth stories, a block-long tramway was built from Washington Avenue. The angle now was quite extreme, and while one man pulled the wheelbarrow another one pushed it from behind. Such backbreaking work! It was impossible to work when the tramway was even slightly dewy or wet because of the danger of slippage. With the completion of the many-windowed fifth story and the monitor roof, the big, bulky mill was finished, at a reported cost of $22,000. The huge building was immediately put to use as a grist and flour mill, droning peacefully on the river bank, turning out up to 120 barrels of flour a day.

In 1862 the mill served as a temporary fortress for worried villagers who feared an Indian attack. In 1881, after a severe winter of heavy snow and a sudden spring thaw, the Cedarburg dam held when all the other dams upstream had given way, and the mill withstood the pounding of the rising waters.

In 1961, the Cedarburg Mill was singled out as a fine example of pioneer architecture and listed on the National Register of Historic Places. Today the historic old mill is still in excellent condition, in use as a feed mill, grinding corn and oats.

As for Burghard Weber, he erected other buildings — homes, hotels, churches — but I believe he always felt that the Cedarburg Mill was his greatest achievement.

■■■

Military Main Street

Jack Rudolph

T he Military Road is gone now, buried under federal, state, county, and town roads that sprawl across the map like a lively mass of worms escaped from their can. One hundred forty years ago, however, a road map of Wisconsin would have shown only a few straggling lines radiating to nowhere from the handful of frontier settlements on the state's fringes. A single trace ran from Green Bay's Fort Howard to Prairie du Chien's Fort Crawford, with but one settlement — Portage — between. That lonely line was the Military Road, and its construction by the United States Army in 1835 through 1837 was one of the most significant events in Wisconsin history.

For nearly twenty years after Fort Howard was established, in 1816, land traffic into the interior was nonexistent. The army posts of Fort Snelling, in Minnesota, and Fort Crawford quickly followed, but their axis of communication was the Mississippi River. The small outpost of Fort Winnebago, at Portage, was the sole break in the Wisconsin wilderness, and it could be reached only by water.

The northern half of the state was blanketed by a dense belt of virgin pine and hardwoods, an almost impassable barrier cut by the Fox and Wisconsin rivers. Except for a few dimly blazed trails only an Indian could follow, land travel was impossible. Travelers dared not leave the rivers, for the forest could swallow a person forever almost within sight of the banks. And even travel by waterways was no picnic. Travelers on both the Fox and Wisconsin were plagued by rapids, sandbars, low water in summer, and ice in winter. Progress was arduous, especially against the current. In addition, the winding riverine routes were much longer than practicable land passages would've been.

By 1825 there were thriving settlements in the lead-mining district of southwestern Wisconsin and at Green Bay, but nothing was known of the country between. Active interest in building a road to connect the two areas began well before 1830. A prime instigator was Judge James Duane Doty, who not only was weary of the tedious canoe trips between regions to hold court sessions but also was intrigued by all that unclaimed real estate.

In 1829 Doty, Henry S. Baird, and Morgan L. Martin struck out on a cross-country journey from Green Bay to Prairie du Chien. The going was rugged, but they succeeded, the first white men ever to cross Wisconsin from east to west by land. Despite all its hardships, the trip confirmed Doty's belief that an overland route was possible. Back in Green Bay, he redoubled his efforts, convincing and assisting a group of local pioneers to draw up a petition to the federal government for such a road.

For several years the proposal got a cold shoulder from Washington. Having just moved the Oneida Indians from New York to new lands in Wisconsin, the government wanted the interior to remain an Indian preserve. Not until 1832, when the Black Hawk War threw the frontier into a panic, did federal authorities awaken to the advantages of such a road. Pressure from the badly frightened settlers was becoming more strident, and the war emphasized the military value of a roadway. The short campaign also gave a lot of volunteer soldiers their first look at central Wisconsin. Most of them were farm boys. They knew good land when they saw it, and what they saw was good land. Many developed a hankering to homestead in the region.

In July of 1832, Congress appropriated funds to survey a military highway connecting forts Howard, Winnebago, and Crawford. Doty and Lieutenant Alexander Center of the Fifth Infantry drew the assignment. Center provided the topographical know-how, but he had enthusiastic help from Doty. To a land speculator of the latter's caliber, the opportunity was too good to miss. The judge used the project to acquire an unrivaled knowledge of the interior, a knowledge that came in handy in future manipulations. The survey took two years and was completed in 1834.

The Military Road was one of the few roadways in the nation to be built entirely by troop labor. Most of the work was done by the Fifth Infantry Regiment, eight of whose ten companies garrisoned forts Howard and Winnebago. The regimental history shows that from 1833 to 1837, companies A and B were in Chicago at Fort Dearborn; companies C, D, E, and F were at Fort Winnebago; and regimental headquarters and companies G, H, I, and K were at Fort Howard. The only other soldiers involved in the task were units of Colonel Zachary Taylor's First Infantry, which were stationed at Fort Crawford.

There is no detailed account of the actual construction of the Military Road, but it is known that the Howard garrison built south toward Winnebago while the Crawford troops worked east from the Mississippi. The Winnebago details probably worked both ways until they met parties coming from the other direction. Averaging forty men in size, companies from each post were assigned in rotation to prepare stretches of about fifteen miles apiece. They could work only in summer, and each company bivouacked on the job, moving camp as

113

it progressed. When a unit had finished its assigned segment, it was relieved. Each company probably spent from four to six weeks in the field.

Though clearing the route was backbreaking labor, the period on the site afforded excellent training for troops who had little to do in garrison but drill, parade, and carouse in the off-post gin mills. In the wilderness, the men learned to maintain a bivouac, take care of themselves in the field, prepare their own food, and march. Furthermore, all work was done under alert conditions. The Indians were never a problem, but after the Black Hawk scare they weren't trusted, so units in the field maintained combat vigilance.

Even in the best weather, conditions were primitive. Virtually every convenience, every feeding and sanitary facility taken for granted by modern armies was nonexistent then. The troops probably had a couple of cows with them for milk, some beef cattle and hogs to be slaughtered as needed, and rations of salt, flour, bacon, and coffee. The meat supply was supplemented by hunting parties. Theoretically, it was every man for himself. In practice, squads usually pooled their rations, which were prepared by the best cook among them. Even then, results were sometimes awful.

The roughest going was the 125-mile stretch between Green Bay and Portage. This portion was slashed out of a virgin forest dotted with swamps and honeycombed by streams. Because most of the area away from the Fox River was swampy, the road had to hug the bank closely, making it necessary to bridge numerous small tributaries. In the first twenty-four miles, the sweating, swearing soldier-builders spanned fifty-six streams. In contrast, the rest of the way was through relatively open country, along fairly well drained high ground. Being generally free of timber, this land was easier to clear. All that was required was to level underbrush, fell a few trees, and bridge some small creeks. The 110-mile southwestern segment was completed the first summer, but the northeastern half wasn't cleared until 1837.

When finished, the Military Road was not much of a highway, even by standards of the day. It was simply a trace, thirty feet wide and cluttered with stumps, more like a fire lane than a thoroughfare. The troops hacking their way across Wisconsin weren't concerned with the comfort of those who would follow. They were interested only in blazing a passage through the wilderness as quickly as possible. How future travelers negotiated it would be their own problem.

Trees six inches or less in diameter were cut off close to the ground. Larger stumps were left with a clearance of twelve inches. No grading was attempted, and swampy places were roughly corduroyed. Some streams were bridged; others merely had their banks cut down so travelers could splash across. The only portion that even approached

114

being a real road was the fifteen miles cleared by Captain Martin Scott's company of the Fifth Infantry. One of the most colorful characters in the service, Scott was ramrod tough and had a flair for road building. His company did not get by with a slapdash job.

Devoid of drainage, the Military Road was impassable in rainy weather. It was usually churned into deep ruts before it dried out, and was choked with dust in summer. Still, for many years, it was the only overland route across Wisconsin. The air along its right-of-way might be blue with pioneer profanity as travelers fought its stumps and potholes, but they used it. They had to. They were, indeed, eager to test its trials. Well before completion, especially along the more open western portion, pioneer families in covered wagons, pack trains, and herds of cattle were streaming over the road into the interior, turning off as they found suitable homesteads, penetrating farther from the path as the nearby land filled up.

A first priority in a new community was to cut a trace to the Military Road. These first settlements, in turn, spawned others deeper in the wilderness, where the process of creating communication was repeated. Eventually, all those crude wagon tracks found their way to the Military Road, the jugular vein of the extensive highway network of modern Wisconsin.

■■■

My Pa's Livery Stable

Irene Schmidt

a's livery stable was located at what is now 1625 South Sixth Street, but in those days was 615 First Avenue. The building still stands on the west side of the street just north of Mitchell Street in Milwaukee. Pa had horses and vehicles for hire by the day or hour.

There were two high, steel doors at the front entrance of the building. They were open during the day, but locked each night. I can still hear the "klump-klump" of the horses' hooves on the wooden-block street. The building was pale yellow brick and extended from the sidewalk back to the alley. An awning with the words LIVERY STABLE shaded the office in summertime. The larger sections of the building housed Pa's office, the harness room, the wash rack and a winter storage room. A rear ramp led to the horse stable. There were spaces for buggies and carriages, including a phaeton and a surrey, and last but not least, Pa's bus.

Pa's bus was not as large nor as long as today's motor buses. It had two long, bench-type seats which each ran the length of the bus, so that passengers sat facing each other. The driver's seat, with a kerosene lamp at each side, was up high, on the outside of the bus. The entrance/exit was to the rear.

One of the most popular trips at that time was a visit to Holy Hill. How did people get to Holy Hill in the horse and buggy days? Some rode the train and transferred to waiting vehicles at Hubertus; some drove one of the many kinds of horse-drawn conveyances, while others joined a pilgrimage. It was this latter, the pilgrimage, for which Pa furnished the bus and drove the pilgrims to Holy Hill, about 30 miles northwest of Milwaukee. Pa had to get up at three o'clock in the morning to get everything ready for those pilgrimages. Ma saw to it that Pa was ready on time.

Frank and Tom, a team of heavy black horses, were fed, neatly curry-combed, and hitched up to the bus. Pa took his seat up front, and with reins in his hands and whip in the socket, proceeded to pick up the pilgrims at a near-by church. After loading the bus (lunch baskets included), they started on their all-day journey and arrived back in Milwaukee late at night.

Pa's office in the livery stable was neat with simple furnishings: a roll-top desk, a swivel chair with arm rests, several straightback chairs and a safe. The roll-top desk had lots of compartments and pigeonholes where daily orders and letters were kept; four drawers on each side with a knee-hole space; a flat surface on which to write; and two shelves that could be pulled out as an arm or leg rest. The roll-top could be lowered and a key turned to lock the desk. A wall telephone was near the desk. It had a crank on its side which had to be turned to get the operator. The number was given. After the call was completed, the crank had to be turned again to let Central know the line was clear. Pa's telephone number was South 328. There were times when orders could not be filled and it was customary for one liveryman to call another to fill the order.

Each summer we looked forward to our annual outing at Muskego Lake, about 12 miles west of Milwaukee. Several other families went with us. Lunch baskets and fishing gear were packed and we were on our way in Pa's bus, which, on family outings, my brother got to drive. Along the way we stopped at a horse-watering trough where the horses could quench their thirst. Heading west on the old Janesville Plank Road, we soon reached a tollgate where Pa paid the toll — one cent per mile for every animal-driven vehicle. After a few friendly words with the tollkeeper, we continued our journey to the lake, where a reserved shady section awaited us. The horses were unhitched and driven to a stable where they rested and were fed. After a day of fishing, picnicking, swimming, wading and rowing, it was time to leave for home, making sure that the big mess of fish we had caught did not get left behind.

Pa's carriage and phaeton were very much alike, with a team of well-groomed horses providing the horsepower. The carriage was used for weddings and funerals, while the phaeton was used for pleasure trips. Its top could be taken off or rolled back. Both vehicles had two seats where the passengers sat facing each other, and each was equipped with elegant kerosene lamps at each side of the driver's seat.

The top-buggy, a one-horse vehicle, was a favorite among young people, and a common mode of transportation for salesmen. Its wooden wheels had no "give" though, and dirt roads could be very bumpy. The surrey, with a fringe on top, was a family conveyance drawn by a team of horses. The seats were nicely upholstered. The polished fenders added beauty to this vehicle.

The harness room was indispensable to Pa's livery business. A lot of space was needed to hang the harnesses up on pegs. Very often they needed repairs. Then too, there were bridles, bits, blinkers, reins, collars and other accessories which had to be kept in place.

The wash rack was where horses as well as vehicles got regular baths. A metal currycomb was used to comb the horses and to remove dirt to improve their appearance. Brushes, chamois and sponges were used to clean the vehicles and then they were polished till they sparkled. Only then were they made available for hire. The stable also had space for storing winter conveyances. There were cutters and a hack-sleigh with bells. A hack-sleigh was a carriage on runners which made it easier for the horses to pull. A foot-warmer and blankets were available on request.

Then, too, the horses had to have their shoes replaced regularly, a job that required skill and was done by a blacksmith whose shop was around the corner near Second and Lapham streets. The blacksmith usually had an audience of children who stood in the doorway listening to the hissing sound of the hot iron and the cling-clang of hammer against anvil.

A rear ramp led down to the horse stable on the ground floor of Pa's building. This floor was covered with heavy planking almost a foot wide. Each horse had his individual stall so as not to kick his stablemates. A rear door led to the alley. There were two long boxes on each side of the door to hold refuse. The horses were bedded with wood shavings and the floors were cleaned several times a day. The boxes were never full for very long because farmers would stop to load the manure onto their wagons and then drive back to their farms where they made good use of the fertilizer.

My favorite horses were Dave, Topsy, Frank, and Tom. Dave, a dapple-grey, was very gentle. He was like a pet to all the children, and the ladies loved him. Topsy, a sorrel, and very intelligent, usually pulled lightweight vehicles. Frank and Tom, the beautiful black

118

horses, always worked together as a team, pulling heavy loads.

In 1904, Pa decided to sell out. He and Ma wanted to retire to a place in the country, so he bought a farm in Franklin. I graduated from Oakwood High School, and the family drove to the graduation exercises in the surrey with the fringe on top. The top, with the fringe, is still in my family.

■■■

Papa and His Ford

Gladys Elviken

P apa loved his Model T Ford. He was a violin maker and he used to drive to town three or four times a week to the express office because violins were shipped to him for repair from all over the United States and sometimes Europe. He was a well-known and loved character in town and as he drove about in his Ford with his black Elbert Hubbard tie flapping (the tie style he wore from the day that Elbert Hubbard himself presented him with one after having bought a violin for his daughter) and his rather long silvery hair waving in the wind he was quite picturesque. As he made his way about town, even people who did not know him spoke to the tall man with the limp who had such a genial manner. The policemen always had a friendly greeting even when Papa occasionally went through a red light. He never had an accident though, due perhaps partly to luck and partly to the fact that he seldom went over twenty miles an hour.

Papa's Ford, a black sedan, was the last of the T models made, and it had one feature that other Model Ts did not — a wide yellow stripe which completely encircled it. Papa painted the stripe on shortly after he bought the car. It was just before Christmas and he had been shopping at a grocery store which dealt in all sorts of Norwegian delicacies, cheese, fish, breads. Papa loved to do the buying for the household and he did it on a generous scale. After loading all his purchases in his car, he went back to chat with his friends. There was laughter and joking as was usual when he was around and he was feeling very jolly when he got home. Looking forward to some good cheese on Mama's homemade bread, he went to get the box of groceries from the car. It wasn't there. But he *knew* he had put it in the car. He was about to retrace his steps when he received a telephone call from the owner of another Model T. The man had found a wonderful box in his car, and after a few inquiries he learned that it belonged to my father. He returned the box, stayed to dinner and ultimately became such a good friend that we were always grateful the mistake had been made. The next day, though, Papa painted the yellow stripe around his car, in the belief that the next mistake might not be such a happy one.

I don't believe anyone got more pleasure out of a car than Papa and Mama did from that Ford. Though fifty miles was the farthest we ever ventured from home, what fun we all had. The all-day trips to pick wild grapes (which kept those kegs in the basement filled with delicious home-brewed wine), the visits to relatives on nearby farms. I remember getting up early in the morning, on days when every blade of grass was covered with dew, and the cobwebs hung with pearls, zigzagging along the road, Papa so full of the joy of living, and Mama serenely keeping one eye on the road and one hand ready to come to the rescue if Papa wandered too far off track.

Sometimes Papa and Mama would drive out into the country and camp overnight in the Ford. Papa had had the front seats altered so they could be folded down for sleeping. He and Mama would cook their breakfast outside and have a great adventure even though they were not more than thirty miles from home.

As the years rolled by and parts became scarce, it became increasingly difficult for Papa to get his Ford repaired. But he would have nothing to do with the new and "improved" cars. When he died in 1936, that Model T was as shiny and new-looking as the day he'd bought it.

■■■

Is This Eden?

Buz Swerkstrom

T he city of La Crosse recently adopted an official emblem proclaiming itself "God's Country." Now, that label is applied to dozens of picturesque places — usually by local chambers of commerce trying to lure tourists — but La Crosse may have more right than other communities to claim Divine favor. If we are to believe a nineteenth-century circuit-riding Methodist preacher, La Crosse was within the walls of the original Garden of Eden.

The idea of Adam and Eve making their home in the Middle West rather than the Middle East sounds a bit preposterous today, but to the Reverend D.O. Van Slyke of Galesville, the notion seemed natural. Having read the Bible from cover to cover "no less than 25 times" without finding a single pasasge that revealed the location of the Garden of Eden, Van Slyke gradually made the "discovery" that the land surrounding him fit the biblical description of Eden almost perfectly. He made his opinion public in a forty-page pamphlet first published by the Galesville Independent Printing House in 1886. Called simply "Garden of Eden," it carries a somewhat more lengthy name on the title page: "Found at Last: The Veritable Garden of Eden, Or a Place That Answers the Bible Description of the Notable Spot Better Than Anything Yet Discovered." Reprinted four times since, the short tract has brought Galesville more publicity than anything else ever said or written about the small town.

"Twenty-seven miles long, five miles wide at each end, and nine miles through the center," Van Slyke's Garden of Eden is located in a bluff-walled valley on the eastward bank of the Mississippi River between La Crosse and Fountain City. This fertile area, he said, offered an infinite variety of wonderful scenery, natural protection from cyclones and earthquakes, and a central location from which Mankind could easily branch out in every direction by following the network of rivers.

Because Adam and Eve wore not so much as fig leaves during their years in Paradise, it's always been hard to imagine the Garden of Eden in the changeable Wisconsin climate, especially during the frigid winter months. The weather was no barrier to Van Slyke's belief, however. "Where would a scientist place the first pair to acclimate?" he asked. "Not too far north, not too far south," he added, answering his own question. He also thought that Paradise "should be destitute of money and mineral wealth, as these, if easily obtained, are corrupting in their tendencies, and should be sought and toiled for to be properly enjoyed." Again, Galesville suited the requirement.

The main part of Van Slyke's argument, though, is based on the geographic structure of the region, which, he says, conforms with the account of the Garden of Eden given in the Old Testament. Citing Genesis 2:8-14 about how "a river went out of Eden to water the garden and from thence it was parted and became into four heads," Van Slyke contended that the Trempealeau, Black, La Crosse, and Mississippi rivers were the only four rivers on earth that came together in the right way. Although the Bible names the rivers Pison, Gihon, Hiddekel, and Euphrates, the minister maintained that was irrelevant. The important point, he argued, was their physical relationship. "The names given to the rivers and places in connection with the original habitation of man," he explained, "were naturally washed out by the flood, or their recollection continued in names of similar places on the new continent."

This explains why Wisconsin is not known as the cradle of civilization. Noah's Ark was at sea for 150 days — long enough to carry surviving humanity to Mt. Ararat, half a world away. It was natural, Van Slyke wrote, "that God should remove the redeemed ones far away from the scenes and remembrances before the Flood, and let him develop up anew... until the sufficient development of his being to allow, by slow stages, to return him to the place of commencement."

Van Slyke, in fact, had an explanation for everything. To those who protested that his Garden was too large, he replied: "Bless you!...Why, did you think the Garden of Eden was only a half acre garden patch, or a small orchard?...How could you get four rivers into it then, to water it, and one of them a Euphrates? (which means long river)...Please just think again, how God had created the whole earth for the habitation of the human family, and would he stint the allotment of the first pair?"

To prove that his was "a land flowing with milk and honey," he listed the prizes won by Wisconsin dairy products at various fairs and international exhibitions. The serpent that tempted Eve to commit the first sin was easy to account for. His "Hanging Gardens," a crescent bluff northwest of Trempealeau that offered a panoramic view of the beautiful river-fed valley, had been "notable and notorious for rattlesnakes from time immemorial." And when Adam and Eve had tasted of the fruit of evil, they were driven out of the Garden westward into the less-irrigated Minnesota (which sounds perfectly logical to

123

Wisconsinites).

Van Slyke's contemporaries considered him a crank, and people in Galesville take him even less seriously today, but it should be remembered that a hundred years ago the location of the Garden of Eden was still a matter of serious debate among some theologians. One thought it was in a "riverless Syrian desert" (as Van Slyke characterized the claim). Another believed it was in a "Florida malarial swamp." Even such a learned man as Boston University President W.J. Warren suggested that it may have been at the North Pole, though he was probably being satirical. Dismissing these theories as patently ungrounded, Van Slyke challenged the world to disprove his own theory, saying that he had presented "an hypothesis that explains all the phenomena and contradicts every opposing hypothesis" and would consider it proof until someone proposed a more convincing case for another locale.

Although he appears to be deadly serious in his claim, there are a few places in the booklet where readers might wonder whether the old minister had his tongue in his cheek while he was writing. Consider this paragraph, for instance: "Did a lawyer from this place make a point in his plea before the court at Whitehall by declaring that I must be mistaken in my locality of the Garden of Eden, for the lack of a personal Devil? In retort, I am compelled to say that I was sent a missionary to this region over 30 years ago, and I found the Devil, or his tools, then predominating in the Methodist Episcopal Society here; and when we tried to turn the rascals out we found that he or they outnumbered us in influence and facilities, and turned the scale against us; and we have abundant facts to show that he has held his grip in that society unto this day."

Whether serious or tongue in cheek, Van Slyke's pamphlet is still a stirring panegyric on the scenery of this pastoral portion of western Wisconsin. "Galesville," he wrote, "is the joy of all its inhabitants, if not of all the earth....Of the scenery we have never tired. It is always fresh and enchanting....O, what a delightful home!" At several places in the book, he invites readers to come and see for themselves: "Here is room for hundreds of thousands of the fallen sons of God to come and regain a home in this Paradise on earth." Lest anyone should accuse him of being a real estate speculator, he was quick to add: "All the land I own is a burial lot in the Galesville cemetery, and not for sale."

His grave can still be found on the brow of the cliff in that cemetery, now known as Pine Cliff Cemetery. He lies beneath a rough stone marker that overlooks his beloved valley, no doubt content to be resting in Eden.

■■■

Chickens and Sausage

Wanda Aukofer

F riday was always Chicken Day. That's because to most people, Sunday dinner meant chicken, and Father was a butcher. So on Fridays our whole family pitched in to prepare chickens and make sausage for Saturday's buying trade.

The butcher shop was at the front of the red brick building we lived in. The basement was as large as the store above it. At the foot of the basement stairs was the "Chicken Room," with two huge barrels, a chopping block (an old tree stump), and a hatchet honed to a sharp edge stuck into the stump. A large icebox that held about 400 pounds of ice was in the front of the basement. Opposite the icebox was a stove with two wash boilers filled with boiling water to dip the beheaded chickens in. In the center of the room there was a long table with benches where we children sat and plucked chicken feathers. About three inches of sawdust covered the floor with an even thicker layer near the chopping block. After the work was done, the debris was shoveled away and clean sawdust put down. I can still smell the sawdust clean and fresh like trees after a summer rain, mixed in with the putrid smell of soggy feathers.

Next to the Chicken Room was the Sausage Room, a smaller room with a wooden floor that was scrubbed and kept immaculate as was the hand-turned sausage grinder and the butcher-block table where other meats were cut up. Father was very fussy and clean about all his meat and took special pride in making his sausages.

On Friday we raced home from school. We knew what a messy, gory job lay ahead of us, but we were all in it together and the shenanigans we pulled when Father wasn't looking made it seem less a chore. My older brother and sister, me, and two or three cousins would go down into the basement wearing long white butcher aprons. We had to be careful not to trip over them. We went down the steps giggling and pushing one another to get a better look at Father chopping off the chickens' heads. Some of the neighbor children were usually peering through the open windows watching him, too. The chickens in their crates were cackling and squawking as though they knew what was coming.

Father deftly grabbed a chicken out of the crate by its feet, put the head on the chopping block, and — whack! — the head fell into the thick sawdust. He threw the fluttering chickens into one of the barrels until the barrelful of beheaded chickens quieted down. Then he dipped them in boiling water and put them on the table for us to pluck. Before long we were throwing handfuls of feathers at each other. Father would admonish us, but one scolding was seldom enough to make us stop.

Sometimes when he was distracted by our horseplay, Father would miss the barrel, and the bouncing chicken would flutter all over the basement splattering blood on the walls, scattering sawdust, flapping in the air. Then bedlam would break loose as we tried to catch the chicken. We children screamed and ran about, bumping into each other, falling into the sawdust, looking much like the chicken we were trying to catch. Father would finally grab a bushel basket to trap the chicken and when he caught it at last, would keep it under the basket until it stopped fluttering.

When the chickens were all cleaned, plucked, and washed, their legs were tied and they were hung on hooks in the big basement icebox, ready for Saturday's rush of business. Then Father went upstairs to clean up before beginning his sausage-making. He put on a snowy white apron and carefully looked over the meat Mother had cut up for sausage, making sure there was no fat on it. We children were supposed to begin cleaning the Chicken Room, but my older brother Ray, about fourteen at the time, was full of mischief and loved teasing us. His teasing usually amounted to no more than a few handfuls of feathers down the backs of our necks, except for the time he instigated the chicken-head war.

As soon as Father left, Ray picked up a couple of bloody chicken heads and threw them at us and at the kids in the windows. We had been tickling each other with wet feathers, but when Ray started pitching the ugly heads about, some of the neighbor kids threw them back. We tried to duck the flying chicken heads and all hell broke loose as we got full of sawdust and feathers trying to get under the table and out of the way. The screaming, shouting, and squealing was deafening. When Father shouted angrily from the top of the stairs, "What the devil is going on down there?" we all scrambled to our places. All was silent. Even the kids in the windows disappeared. When Father came down the stairs with a tray of meat for the sausage, Mother right behind him, they looked at the war zone and were stunned. Gingerly watching their step to avoid all the chicken heads on the floor, they placed their trays on the table in the Sausage Room, then came back looking very stern.

"Who started all this?" Father demanded.

Nobody answered. Ray was sitting at the end of the table innocently plucking a chicken. He didn't dare look up.

"If you children won't tell, you will *all* get a licking," Father warned.

We girls knew what we were in for if we tattled on Ray. He would never stop teasing us. But my older sister, more afraid of a licking than of the teasing, said in a shaking voice, "Ray started it. He was throwing chicken heads at us..."

Father grabbed Ray by the arm and, big as my brother was, put him over his knee. Even worse, his punishment included shoveling out the sawdust and litter by himself. I don't remember Ray ever pulling that stunt again!

Father meanwhile washed his hands and again changed his apron so he could begin the sausage making. A meticulous person, everything had to be clean before he started. He checked the casings. The spices had to be measured just so, and the meat weighed precisely. I remember still the aroma of those spices and fresh meat. It was like dried rose leaves, and woodsy sage mixed with pepper, a scent that was flowery but strong.

We children hurried to clean up so we could take turns cranking the sausage grinder. Sometimes the meat had to be ground two or three times to meet my father's standard of perfection. Then he would put the casings on the grinder for filling. It was fascinating to watch the casings fill up with the delicious-smelling mixture. Father showed us how to twist and turn the casings so all the sausages were of uniform size. When the long strings of sausage were finished, we looped them over poles in the icebox. They looked like giant chains.

Come Saturday morning there was fresh sausage for breakfast, and of course for Sunday dinner, the biggest, plumpest chickens. It always seemed that because we had worked so hard on the chickens and sausages, they tasted extra good. If I close my eyes, I can taste them still.

■ ■ ■

Pipe-Organ Pumper

Lorenz Hackbarth

I have something in common with the likes of Bernard Baruch and Andrew Carnegie. I'm eligible for membership in the Guild of Former Pipe-Organ Pumpers, an organization to which those two famous fellows could very well have belonged. The only requirement for membership is that at one time or another you pumped a pipe organ by hand.

When I was a kid there were two churches in Tomah that had pipe organs — St. Paul's (Lutheran) and St. Mary's (Catholic). It was during World War II and I was about 11 years old when I started my job as pumper. My partner at the time was Albert Danus. We would alternate pumping for each hymn on Sundays. It was probably considered good exercise for two big kids.

Being a pumper took a certain amount of concentration, not to mention a strong back. The technique was fairly simple. The old organs had a wooden handle protruding from one side, something like the handles on the old farm pumps. This handle was worked up and down in a slot about two and a half feet long. To one side of the main slot and a bit higher was a narrower slot from which the head of a six-inch screw protruded. This smaller slot had upper and lower marks and the position of the screw head in relation to the marks indicated the amount of air in the bellows.

To assume the proper stature for pumping I'd take a position on the step just below the wooden pump handle. To start off I had to use both hands and pump up and down furiously, all the while keeping a watchful eye on the screw head in the smaller slot. That screw head had to stay above the lower mark of the indicator slot. After warming up, I could alternate hands to relieve my muscles. Woe betide you if you inadvertently let the indicator drop below the lower mark — the organ would emit a wheezing sound like some infirm being. Teachers and church elders were firm believers in the "Spare the rod, spoil the child" theory.

I had to be current on church ritual too, so I could relax a bit during the Gospel and Epistle. There was usually a few seconds after the Amen at the end of the sermon too, but I had to be sure to have a good head of air for all the alleluias and the other responses during the liturgy.

As important as priming the pump organ was proper attire. There was no such thing as comfortable clothes. My Sunday attire, winter or summer, included knee pants, a shirt with a high, stiff, choking celluloid collar, a hook-on tie, a coat, high-button shoes, and long black cotton stockings held up with elastic garters above the knee. (Sixty years later I can still see the constriction marks made by those homemade garters.)

With that uniform and the raised organ/choirloft in the rear of the church it was hot in the summer and hotter in the winter, when the heat from the old wood-fired furnace seemed to stagnate up there. Of course during the sermon it was our privilege to sit on one of the folding chairs and lean back against the stair rail, in company with one of the elders. And there were other rewards too. Sometimes during the school day there would be a wedding or a funeral, and one of us pumpers would have to go and pump the organ.

For all of this we received the magnificent sum of fifty cents per month (a bit more on those lucky occasions when you got a tip for a wedding or a funeral). I never did get around to joining the Guild, but then I guess Baruch or Carnegie never did either.

■■■

Woodstove Winter

Michael Goc

O n a January night so cracking cold that even the trees in the yard sound groans of desperation, I'm roused. It's not the ususal ear-stinging sound of the alarm clock that wakes me but the complaining nerve endings in my nose. They complain because they — we — are cold. I suddenly understand why knitted nose-warmers were so popular in the nineteenth century. I also realize that my wood-burning stove and I are involved in a mutually dependent relationship. My nose and I want heat. The stove wants tending. And so although — or because — the thermometer hanging not so mutely on the wall says 50 degrees, I must leave the bed and flounder to the stove.

Has a too-long log hung up in the firebox? Have I woodenheadedly used a too-green chunk for overnight banking? Has the temperature outside fallen so drastically in the last few hours (this *is* Wisconsin, after all) that the stove's flue requires adjustment?

The questions are superfluous. There is no automatic valve to pour more gas into the burner, no sentrylike thermostat to guard the stability of the room's temperature, not even a rumbling 1930s stoker to feed shining chips of midnight-black coal onto the blaze. There's only me, with my abused nose and clumsy bare feet, stumbling in the dark, opening the ornamented iron door, tending the stove. In the cold, at night, while others sleep uninterrupted in the warmth of central heat, I wonder if I really want a mutually dependent relationship with a numb hunk of iron.

Later, just before the January dawn, breakfast is cooking — on the wood-burning stove. Americans, so they say, don't make breakfast anymore. The hurried tempo of life, commuter living, the delectability of the Egg McMuffin, all have contributed to the decline of home-cooked morning meals. So they say. The truth of the matter is that Americans gave up breakfasts when they gave up wood-burning stoves to cook them on.

Examine this early morning picture. An old-fashioned cookstove — heavy bodied, more doors in its side than a limousine, a woodbox filled with small logs at its flank — is brightly dispersing the dark chill that filtered into the kitchen overnight. Imagine the warm iron stove top, glowing red only at the hot spot over the firebox. The coffee is already perking there. At center stove, pop-eyed eggs fry slowly and evenly because the entire undersurface of the pan is heated. Slightly closer to the hot spot, the bacon, too, sizzles evenly. Flanking the eggs, on the cooler side, is the toast. It's laid out flat on the stove top, a marching row of light bread slowly baking golden. Farther yet to the right is a single coffee cup — my own — kept at just the right temperature by the stove top's generous warmth.

Before it all I stand, an ordinary morning-rumpled man in blue jeans. But with spatula in hand, I am Stokowski conducting Chopin. The overture begins. The toast is half done; flip it over. Bend to check the fire; insert another log; close the flue a bit. Flip the bacon onto a plate and into the warmer atop the stove. There it will stay, moist and warm, until the slow risers dawdle down to snatch it. Sip the coffee; even the bottom of the cup is warm. The toast is ready; set it, too, in the warmer. Finally the eggs are done and slid into the warmer.

Breakfast is ready. But the breakfasters aren't. My morning performance — and the stove's — plays to a house of sleepyheads. But the stove will wait for them, will keep it all warm. I stuff a large log into the firebox, adjust the vent so that heat will be thrown into the oven, and open the oven door to send the heat into the room.

Because the stove is my only company, I reflect on its humble virtues. I'm reminded of the sage who said that there are no new ideas, that the more things change, the more they remain the same. I look at the stove top, the two-foot by three-foot warm slab, and think of a magazine ad trumpeting the latest kitchen innovation. It is a burnerless stove top whose smooth surface can heat quickly in one spot and slowly in another. Just like my cookstove. Above the stove top in the ad is a special feature: a warming oven that can heat rolls and thaw frozen food. Just like my cookstove. On the counter next to the new stove is an automatic coffeemaker proudly guaranteeing a warm cup all morning. Just like my cookstove. My hunk of iron holds its heat for hours and, with the occasional addition of a good log, will stay hot all day. It's a hunk of iron that could bring back breakfast. It's also a hunk of iron, I realize, with which I'm happy to have a mutually dependent relationship.

But the new stove is all automatic, say those whose vision doesn't go beyond the dial that turns the gas on and off. I labor to put wood into my stove; another labors to pay a gas bill. Are we so different?

To say that during a Wisconsin winter there is a great need for heat is to understate the obvious. Not so obvious is the fact that for most of their history, Wisconsin residents have kept themselves warm with wood. And wood — abundant, bulky, beautiful — warms more of us every year. Wisconsin Indians built fires in the centers of each of their shelters and allowed the smoke to find its own way to a hole in the roof. The Indian fire radiated heat all around and filled the upper reaches of the hut with sultry smoke that served both to warm the inhabitants and to preserve the meat and fish strung up in the hazy bath.

Europeans, in the name of cleanliness, invented the chimney. But the gain in neatness was offset by the loss of heat. For even the most soundly constructed modern fireplace sends a full three quarters of its heat to the frigid blue skies above. Although Europeans eliminated the smoke when they threw up their chimneys, they in no way disturbed the only feature of wood heat that is automatic. That is its attraction. Strangers who enter a wood-heated home find themselves magnetically drawn to the stove. It is the center of winter activity, a thing of life radiating waves of comfort. And this comfort is adjusted not by spinning a thermostat but by sliding a chair closer to or further from the fire.

My wife, who, when all is said and done, would rather be in Key West, came home one typical winter day and hurriedly drew a chair up to the parlor stove. There she sat, silently shivering.

"I can tell you must be cold," I remarked brightly.

"How?" she asked, sarcasm in her voice.

"You're sitting so close to the stove you're scorching our antique rocker."

Central heating helped kill the ancient idea that a home has a physical center, an obvious spot from which its winter-bound inhabitants mark off their activities. But put a wood-burning stove in the parlor, and, though it might be hazardous for the furniture, the home will find its center.

There might be places better suited to heating with wood than Wisconsin, but not many. The southern portion of the state, which is an extension of the wood-shy Illinois prairie, and the extreme north, a country of fir and pine, are not the best. But look in the old Driftless Area and in the central region adjacent to it, and there is wood for heating. In every fold of the hills there are hickories and white oaks, whose output of BTUs approaches that of coal. Red oak, hard maples, and birches fill the hills with color and the homes with heat.

If there is a liability to wood heat, it lies in that mutually dependent relationship. If I don't hold up my end, the stove can't hold up its. Sometimes the spontaneous mobility so ordinary in American life is impossible. Weekends away are forgotten if we expect the stove to heat the house. But a sense of weather compensates for automatic valves. Above-zero temperatures mean we can slip away overnight and not return to frozen pipes. Colder weather means we stay at home, by the stove, where we would rather be anyway.

■■■

Dairy Cows and Seed Corn

Margaret H. Holzman

I n 1920, the township of Menasha, like many rural areas, was badly in need of teachers in their one-room elementary schools. So the school board decreed that for one year only, special teaching licenses would be issued to high-school graduates who could pass a qualifying exam.

I was starry-eyed and oh, so young! After all, I had begun teaching my younger sister as soon as she could talk, and I had taught my brother to wipe dishes correctly, much to his disgust. Opportunity was surely knocking!

I arranged to take the test, which would cover fourteen subjects, at Oshkosh. Being a city girl, one subject worried me — agriculture. So I gave myself a crash course on the subject, learning, among other things, the four kinds of dairy cows and how to test seed corn. When I opened the agriculture section of the test and saw that two of the questions were to name the four kinds of dairy cows and tell how to test seed corn, I was sure that destiny was leading me. I passed the exam and was hired. Although I had been advised not to accept less than $90 a month, I hesitated for thirty seconds and grabbed at $85.

The day after Labor Day arrived. I faced my pupils, thirty of them. Twenty-nine were in the eight grades. One girl had graduated the year before, but asked to return for another year. (The fact that her house was near the school and had a handy well in the yard may have influenced the school board.) She was allowed to take a "post graduate" course, and each day one of the bigger boys took a porcelain pail and filled it at her father's well. The pail was set in the back of the room, and all day long thirsty boys and girls drank from the big dipper resting in the water.

Seven of my pupils were first graders. What a thrill it was to hear them reading after a few weeks! But in our seven-hour day, I could devote only four 15-minute periods to them. The only books, outside of their texts, were those I brought from the library each week. So I prepared seatwork for them, which they devoured as baby birds do the food their parents bring. Then they stared at the other classes and wiggled. This listening to other recitations went on all day, with every grade. At first I was perturbed when a seventh grader would wave his hand, wanting oh, so much to answer a question I had posed to the fourth graders. But soon I realized this was to be a fact of life in a one-room school. Before long I had my whole family working nightly to prepare seatwork for all the children.

To get to school in the shortest time, I walked about a mile and a half down the Soo Line tracks. There was an uphill grade for a distance, and an extra engine helped pull freight trains up the hill and then returned to the station area. Whenever my trek home coincided with its return, the engineer would stop and I would clamber up into the cab, try to ignore the noise, and rest my tired feet. I blessed that engineer every time he stopped. Occasionally, a section gang on a handcar would stop for me. I would curl up into a ball and pray that I wouldn't fall off as we zipped down the track lickety-split.

One of my nightly chores was to sweep the unvarnished wood floor of the schoolroom. At first it was easy. But rain and snow made mud on the playground, and that mud caught in the framework of the desks, which were fastened down. Sweeping became an abomination! So I devised a scheme: each night the person in each row who had the most mud under his seat would sweep the row. I would finish the job. This worked like a charm. The older boys invariably became the "row sweepers," and they seemed to accept this small task good-naturedly. For a week I enjoyed my small triumph. Then the blow fell. One morning an angry father of four of my pupils, who was also a member of the school board, appeared. I was hired to sweep the floor, he told me in a loud, petulant voice. What did I mean by assigning part of *my* job to his son George? His haranguing voice drowned my feeble attempts to explain. After he left I had my first chance to refrain from visiting anger at the father on the son. I managed to give George an extra word of praise for a good arithmetic paper. This was a bigger triumph than my short-lived escape from sweeping had been.

This same father appeared frequently during the year. I had let the teeter-totter be broken when two boys were playing on it. I had taught the county health lessons which advocated a weekly bath. I dreaded to see his face. Never, in his estimation, did I do anything right. Yet his four children were learning, and I was proud of their progress.

In one corner of the schoolroom was a wood-burning stove of which I was in sole charge. Persuading that beast to give forth just the right amount of heat was harder than persuading any recalcitrant pupil to toe the mark. One noon in November while my pupils were out playing, the north wind began to howl. I thought the fire had gone out so I threw in some kindling and some kerosene. In a flash I seemed to be enveloped in flames. I rubbed my dress vigorously with my right arm to put out the fire. I rang the bell and told my pupils to please go home. They looked at me horrified. I managed to get home, and my mother looked at me the same way my students had. My eyebrows were burned off and so was the front of my hair. My face was black. My right arm was covered with blisters. The doctor cleaned it and put it in a sling.

Some kind soul drove me to school the next morning. I knew when I left in the morning that I would need a lot of courage to get through the day, but little did I dream what fate had in store for me. At 9:30 the door opened and in walked the county superintendent of schools and my former high-school principal. They were there to "inspect" me. They stayed all morning. I still believe that my obvious discomfort resulted in a more merciful judgment than I might otherwise have received. At any rate, there was no knock on the door the next morning, and no loud voice telling me I wouldn't do as a teacher.

The days flew by: a Christmas party, a box social, Valentines exchanged, blizzards when walking was very difficult (school was never closed), then beautiful, balmy days, and finally county tests for sixth, seventh, and eighth graders, which they all passed, glory be! Then, suddenly, it was the last day of school and time for our traditional events: a picnic for parents and children, and final report cards.

In my considered judgment (I was all of nineteen years old), all but one of my pupils were ready for the next grade. One sweet little first-grader, very immature, had stayed home most of the year. When she returned, she could "read" her book from cover to cover, but she didn't know a single word in it. With her mother's help, she had memorized it. The day of the picnic the pressure began. Her grandfather was president of the school board. Her uncle was my loud-voiced early morning visitor. The county superintendent of schools was there

136

and was the recipient of some of the pressure. Even he finally asked me if I could reconsider. But I stuck to my decision. Years later I thought of how stubborn I was, but my ideals were high, and I did what I felt was right.

It had been a good year, and I had learned a lot more than just the four kinds of dairy cows and how to test seed corn. After four years of college I went back to teaching with a few more skills, but not with any more enthusiasm or love for my pupils than I had that first year.

■■■

House to House

Barbara Lunenschloss

S mall towns produce memorable characters in each generation, well-known to everyone because they are such an integral part of daily life. Montfort in the early twenties was no exception. There was the ragman, a kindly bearded fellow who made his way door to door with his wares flung over his shoulder. My sister and I looked forward to his visits. He would weigh our sack of goods on his spring scale and announce how much he would give us in trade (anywhere from ten to thirty cents' worth); we were then allowed to choose from his supply of graters, tin cups, corkscrews, combs, strainers, and the like. Besides the ragman there was usually an assortment of tramps who came to our door too. In those days tramps were fed instead of feared.

But the character I remember most vividly was an amiable local peddler with the unusual name of Grant House. This little fellow with his reddish hair and mustache came often enough to be classed as a pest by the heads of some households, but to my sister and me he was a source of entertainment and of a wondrous variety of interesting merchandise, and we welcomed his arrival. We would spy him turning Bennie Cook's corner a half block away. In his shiny black suit, black felt hat, and narrow buttoned shoes which turned up at the toes like elves' slippers, he was indeed hard to miss. He carried a large black satchel filled with his products, and was always on foot because the first time out with his Maxwell Runabout, he had lost control of the monster and he was never able to summon enough courage to take it out again.

Grant would rap at our door and sing out, "Mornin' Bess! Need anything today?" Without waiting for an invitation to come in, he would open the door and before Mother had a chance to say no, he would launch into the same sales pitch he used every week. It was routine to start out with the mundane kitchen products.

"Need any vanilly? Cinnamon? Nutmeg?" and on down the list until he had exhausted it and also himself, because he had stopped for neither breath nor an answer. He would grab a quick breath and almost immediately go into a spiel for his cosmetic line. This particular sales pitch was a source of great amusement to my sister and me. Little snickers would begin escaping from the corners of our mouths almost before he began, and became increasingly difficult to stifle.

"Got some mighty good-smelling Lilac Kologny," he'd say. A stern look from Mother and we would try to straighten our faces. But by the time he got to the "Traveling Ar*buttus*" we would be convulsed with laughter, tears running down our cheeks and Mother glaring at us. So I'd cough hard and blow my nose as though I had a cold. One look at me and Grant would reach into his black satchel and with the air of a great physician push a jar into my mother's hands, saying, "Bess, that girl's got an awful cold. Take this cold cream and rub it on her forehead and chest each night. Best cure there is." Mother would thank him graciously and assure him that she would apply it as long as needed.

Sometimes Grant would have something really special in his bag, like the time when, with a gleam in his eye, he gingerly unfolded a piece of tissue paper and there lay the filmiest, loveliest hosiery we had ever beheld. With greatest pride he announced, "*Chif*fon Hose." My sister, who was just beginning to notice boys, and vice versa, looked longingly at the hosiery. No doubt envisioning her lanky legs swathed in those revealing stockings, she finally persuaded Mother to help her become a sex symbol, and for the next week we ate tasteless cookies minus "vanilly."

Usually, by the time Grant had exhausted his list, he had exhausted Mother's patience and her secret fund in the little china sugar bowl as well. So with a jaunty, "Thank ya, Bess! See ya next week!" he would pick up his black satchel and with a doff of his hat was off to our neighbors'.

Today peddlers like Grant House live only in memories of an era of kerosene lamps, crank phones, filmy chiffon hose, and the scent of lilac "kologny."

■■■

Ode to Overalls

Justin Isherwood

T here have been, in the course of things, odes to love and larks, to ladies, to athletes dying young, to melancholy and flowers. But there has never been an ode to bib overalls.

Sometimes known as bibs, baggies, and farmer clothes, in the townships, they are simply overalls (pronounced *overhauls*). They seem little more than a pair of extra-long potato sacks, yet share the same sense of design usually reserved for expensive motorcycles, military aircraft, and proposals of marriage. They are the costume of most farmers, some railroaders, and a few truck drivers. For the farmer, they are the self-explanatory sign of vocation; they define adequately the creature caged within.

Unlike blue jeans, which are comfortable and stylish enough for the movie house if not the church, bib overalls are made for one thing: work. They are properly worn long, so the pants drape like Indian leggings over the shoes, thus keeping the toes polished and the laces clean. The deep cuffs short-circuit sandburs, snow, and dog bites, and permit several subsequent shortenings before the boot top is surpassed or the overalls are handed down to some junior partner with shorter legs. The curious shapes and sizes of patches — necessarily double-stitched — on a pair of overalls tell of affairs with welders and over-exuberant attempts to leap a barbed-wire fence, the top strand of which is nearly always an inch too high and wholly unforgiving. Pole vaulters may have farther to fall, but barbed-wire jumpers expose the undercarriage to greater risk.

Overalls come in different colors — all variations of blue — and have the virtue of not showing dirt. Some have longitudinal white lines over the blue, but these are generally considered too fancy for work. Some are a blue so thick it appears almost black. Worn daily, these become, in time, a faded, brittle blue, the color of the sky. Manufacturers could have made overalls brown or green, but then the farmer wearing them might disappear altogether against new-plowed fields or summer pastures.

It's hard to get the overalls off once the man is in harness, but it *is* permissible to change to a clean pair if headed for the hardware

140

store. Country wives acquire milers' lungs from hollering after pickup trucks pointed toward town — questioning the cleanliness of the drivers' attire. The urgency of the errand determines whether or not the truck turns around.

Some farmers wear jeans underneath their overalls; some, the customary cottons; others, just what comes natural. It's a seasonal decision. In late October, a man might wear a voting majority of his wardrobe: jeans, long johns, wool pants, overalls. And a wool coat. It takes awhile for rain to soak through a half-inch-thick wool coat. With his coat double-buttoned and collar up, wearing a hat with earflaps down, a man has the appearance of a displaced tar-paper fishing shack set atop a tractor seat.

July is an altogether different territory. Propriety, modesty, appearance, be damned. Come July, with its chafe of combining and haying, manners move over. Overalls are worn circus-tent style, loose and floppy, giving the semblance of shelter but not hiding much. On humid afternoons, when the air is as thick as a lump of melting butter, the three brass side buttons arbitrate between decency and its detour. Forsaking linen linings to let the breezes enter the inner reaches of those overalls may be downright indecent, but then, so is July.

Bib overalls are something of a cross between jeans and a blacksmith's apron. Mark Twain doubted the morality of their design, thinking the bib appendage was inclined to hide more than a dirty shirt. True, the bib does make it possible to rest your arms and get a scratch in without dislodging decorum. Neighbors, when they meet at fence lines, can be seen talking, shoulders tilted against fence posts, arms tucked into bibs. I suspect the design of their clothes enhances the peaceful nature of their discussion.

Of pockets, overalls have a sheer selfish monopoly. No fishing-tackle box, tool chest, or post office has more pigeon holes. A person could lose half a day looking for a lock washer sequestered earlier — but where? When a bib-overalled customer comes in, store clerks learn to look busy, fearful he'll disrupt business by frisking himself right there in front of everybody while searching for his checkbook or billfold, dreading what he might pull out because it felt like a change purse.

Depending on how you count, there are twelve or thirteen pockets in a pair of bibs. The right front pants pocket is more a badger hole, though. It can swallow an arm to the elbow or a ten-inch crescent wrench, whole. Rumor is, it can also conceal a sectioned fishing pole and fly reel, revealing nothing of the day's diverted destiny. Or it might hold a novel or a magazine to read under a shade tree when mowing becomes too boring or too hot. Or a Thermos of lemonade, swimming trunks, and a towel.

141

Below this first large receptacle are two pockets sewn one atop the other, pliers pockets, for two pairs of pliers. (One might wear out or get lost, or you might lend one to a neighbor.) Behind, there's a hip pocket about the size of a stop sign, designed to hold work gloves (two pairs) or a set of socket wrenches or a tire iron or an afternoon's supply of fence staples.

The left front pocket is just as deep as its right-hand counterpart. Deep enough for bolts, nails, wirecutters, and a couple lengths of repair boards. Things can get lost in there, which makes you kind of afraid to poke your hand in, not quite remembering all that has been inserted over the last week. If it is a wife's duty to clear out the aliens therein, a smart woman learns to look before setting the contents loose to rattle around in the washing machine. Even smarter wives write off the machine, not wishing to risk a hand to what might be waiting in the pocket's depths, a ferocity of random design fashioned from bits of barbed wire, screws, and eight-penny nails. Or a slimy stinkhorn mushroom, put there by a practical joker of a husband, whose image of her jerking her hand out nervous and quick, face flushed hot, is enough to keep him going all morning.

Below the left front pocket is the hammer loop. The hammer feels odd, like a long-barreled gun, but it makes a man feel functional. Unfriendly dogs go for the hammer handle and hang on, which does little for the life of the loop or the intended trajectory of the wearer.

An oil rag, a couple handfuls of new potatoes, or a supper's worth of sweet corn can fit comfortably in the left hip pocket. Not only is there room enough for nearly everything in those hip pockets, but it's possible to sit down without crushing, suffocating, or even feeling whatever is in them — oil can, spare headgasket, or baby chicken. Don't ask how.

The bib is a complication of pockets: two snap pockets, one watch pocket, one pencil pocket, and one eyelet for a watch fob. Bib pockets tell pretty much what there is to know about a man. If he chews, the outline of his snuff-box is a ghost of a moon on the bib front. If he smokes a pipe, the stem sticks out of a snap pocket. Some keep a notebook to remember when they planted corn, when it rained last, how much the fertilizer cost a year ago, a nephew's birthday, or when the Holstein third from the end last came in heat.

The bib is an outright display of where a person has been and where he's going. Even religious beliefs can be ascertained. Where fingers have worn a path of habit and devotion, there's a pale tracing of a cross. If he is a freethinker, that too shows; fishhooks snagged in the threads indicate other methods of Sunday-morning meditation. The bib is the place in which to carry home pinecones or a baby kitten, the place where kids search for candy, new marbles, salesmen's pencils,

142

and allowance money.

The thirteenth pocket is front center, three buttons. It is known in the townships as the Saturday-night pocket, the first day of creation, and grandpa's retirement plan.

Overalls are to the farmer what armor was to the crusader, an exoskeleton, a fortress. They hold the farmer up when his body feels like a stone from lugging oats to a second-floor granary. They are a lifeboat when, marooned by storm or breakage, he finds tucked in a pocket a newspaper clipping, a sonnet, or a pouch of tobacco, cob pipe, and kitchen match.

A grandfather's overalls hang from a whitewashed timber in the cow barn. The wind through Dutch doors shakes them; a pocketful of bolts from some forgotten chore weighs them down. A pipe stem — calumet of the township, peace arbiter of early frost and slammed doors — sprouts from a bib pocket. Unnotified of the man's change of address to a smaller plot of ground, the overalls seem memory and memorial enough, the tabernacle of a way of life.

■■■

Two Christmas Vignettes

I

Eleva D. Heimbruch

We were rural folks who celebrated Christmas not so much with monetary gifts as with gifts of our time, our talents, and ourselves. The most meaningful Christmas of our lives came during the Depression. Everyone, it seemed, was poor. Our little daughter was three years old and the thought of no presents for her was unbearable. Things looked bleak. Then an idea took shape in my head and with it came a glimmer of hope.

I gathered handfuls of the bright orange bittersweet that grew in abundance in our woods, along the way picking wild grass, weeds and milkweed pods from the fields and fence rows. These I arranged into lovely winter bouquets. For the vases I chose any bottle, jug, or container with an interesting contour, to which I pasted small bits of brightly colored paper. Then I coated each with a thin layer of shellac. With more than a few misgivings I took my homemade merchandise to New London to sell door-to-door.

A Divine Hand must surely have given compassionate guidance to the ones who opened their doors to me that day. Or perhaps they sensed the quiet desperation of the unusual peddler who rang their doorbells. I shall forever be grateful to those kind souls who made possible my purchase of a few luxuries: fruit, candy and nuts, some crayons and coloring books and a very precious doll.

From my husband's skillful hands came a tiny cradle with a bright coat of paint. That cradle and doll became our little girl's most prized possessions.

■■■

II

Gladys M. Rebelein

As twilight deepened into darkness that late December afternoon, and the last few snowflakes fluttered to the snow-covered farmyard, my father smiled. "It is always good to have a little more snow, to insure good sleighing all winter," he murmured. "We must hurry with our chores," he continued, "for we do not want to be late for the Christmas program."

We children didn't need any reminder. Hadn't we practiced our songs and recitations every Sunday after Sunday School? Hadn't we stood still, or at least tried, while Mother patiently fitted our new clothes? Those Christmas clothes were something very special. One wore them first to the program, and then every Sunday until Easter. Last year's Christmas dress became a school dress to be worn every day, with a pinafore apron over it, and changed as soon as one came home from school. We knew that, even now as we were talking, Mother was carrying from the closet all of our new clothes and laying them out on our beds. But there was no time for daydreaming. There were chores to be done.

One of us had to crawl up into the silo to throw down the silage, while someone carried the sour smelling stuff to the cows, waiting patiently in their stanchions. Then the ground grain had to be portioned out to each one. This was done very carefully according to the reward system. Daisy received two canfuls because she was a good producer, while Big Red got only one.

The horses, too, had to be fed according to the amount they deserved. That was more fun because ear corn was easier to carry, as was a bit of oats, and a big forkful of hay. Besides, the horses always stuck out their noses for a pat, and often we dared ourselves to hold out the ears of corn while they grabbed it from our hands. That night two of them got a few extra loving pats. Weren't they the ones that were going to take us to church?

In the meantime, someone had to feed the pigs and chickens. We all helped milk cows. The cats sat close, knowing that their pans would soon be filled with warm, fresh milk. Last of all hay had to be thrown down for morning. That was fun too. Sometimes the cats followed us up the short ladder to the mow. In a bit of high-spirited teasing, we stuffed a little hay down each other's necks, then threw down forkful after forkful to the floor below, until even Father decreed that it was enough. Then came the thrill of jumping down into the big pile of hay.

We hurried through our supper of fried potatoes, cheese, sauce canned the previous summer, and some Christmas cookies. The dishes too were washed quickly. We checked to be sure there was plenty of warm water in the reservoir of the old wood-and-coal-burning stove to wash ourselves with. Perhaps ears and necks were washed just a bit more carefully that night, but nevertheless, one basin of water had to be enough for all five of us. Water had to be carried by the pailful from the well, which was a long ways from the house, so it was used sparingly.

The sleigh had already been covered with a layer of straw that afternoon, and the horses had been harnessed, but not hitched. It was only a matter of minutes until the tugs were hooked to the bobsled and the neckyoke put in place. This was a special night so sleigh bells were strapped around each horse's belly.

Mom brought out the soapstone which had been heating in the oven and we two older children each carried out a horsehide robe. We children and Mom sat facing each other in the sleigh, our feet and legs crossing in the middle, each of us trying to get our feet nearer the soapstone. We placed the heavy robes across our laps. Father, in his big sheepskin coat, stood at the front and drove the horses. If he became too chilled, he would clap his hands while holding the reins, or sometimes even jump out and run alongside the sleigh.

"Let's stop and pick up our cousins too," we yelled. "It will be fun." We all shoved together a little closer. The boys would have liked to show off a bit and run beside the sleigh, but our mothers forbade it on this night, when appearance was important.

The four miles to church were covered long before we had run out of chatter. Women and children were let out at the church door, while fathers drove their teams to the sheds in the parking lot. My father's shed was Number 22 and for that he paid a certain amount of rent each year. Once inside we took off our heavy coats and boots while our mothers tried to brush our hair a bit and straighten shirts and dresses, all the while secretly hoping that no restroom trips would be necessary before the program was over. The "restrooms" were way out beyond the horse sheds, and a trip there meant putting on coats and boots and going out into the dark.

Somehow each of us children managed to get through our part of the program without too many mistakes. We felt very special in our new clothes. The sparkle of excitement in the eyes of the very little children was almost brighter than the candles lighting the huge tree. Then it was gift time. There was a sack filled with Christmas goodies for each of us, and a gift under the tree from our Sunday School teacher, and maybe even a present from a cousin or a friend.

Finally it was all over, the Christmas hymns, the blessing, the final "Merry Christmas" called out to friends as sleighs departed. The sleigh was cold and so was the straw, and the soapstone had long since ceased to give out warmth. But it didn't matter. Our hearts were warm and gay, and only the littlest went to sleep.

■■■

Mark It Paid!

William E. Daley

I was a newsboy some sixty years ago in North Lake, a Waukesha County village nestled at the northern end of picturesque Pine and Beaver lakes in the famed Kettle Moraine area. There was more to being a newsboy then than just tossing a newspaper on a front porch. Delivering the paper was a mission that required a special knowledge of customers and their eccentricities. A bit of finesse and diplomacy paid off handsomely.

The nearby metropolitan newspaper, *The Milwaukee Journal,* was the most widely read newspaper in our thriving farming community. In the early years of the twentieth century, the *Journal* arrived daily from the big city via the Milwaukee and St. Paul railroad, a one-track service that terminated in North Lake. It was tagged in its later declining years with the moniker "bugline" because the train crawled along at fifteen miles an hour due to warped rails and a roller coaster roadbed.

At the turn of the century, however, the railway line did a booming business in freight and passenger service. Ice harvested on North Lake was shipped in carload lots to Milwaukee and Chicago. Shipment of grain and feed was a flourishing business. Passenger service, predominantly salesmen and businessmen, was brisk. Wealthy people from Milwaukee and Chicago commuted to the popular summer lake resorts. Newsboys gathered at the depot each day, subbed the sections and made deliveries. Sunday paper mishaps occurred occasionally when bundles, errantly tossed before the train had slowed sufficiently, were sucked under the wheels, ground to bits and scattered by the wind.

When I took over one of the *Journal* routes, I soon discovered that I was no longer the free and easygoing lad who never missed a chance at a pickup ball game, tag, hide-and-seek, pom-pom-pullaway, or run-sheep-run. My customers depended on the *Journal* for their daily news. When I didn't deliver the paper on time, a telephone call to my parents followed. I soon learned it was safer for my health and happiness to peddle the paper on schedule. Of course, I couldn't blame my customers for wanting punctuality. The *Journal* was their primary source of world and state news. There was no television and very few families owned radios.

By the end of World War I, electricity had come to North Lake and the price of the daily *Journal* had risen from two cents to three cents. The Sunday edition had gone up from five cents to ten cents. With the growth of the automobile came an influx of "summer" people to the nearby lakes, and the newsboys' business boomed. We expanded beyond the village limits and delivered papers to the lake resorts. This more than doubled our normal winter business. Sundays were especially lucrative when we dared to order a hundred extra *Journals,* haul them to the steps of the local churches and sell them to the standing-room crowds as they left services.

The extra income I was earning required, at my parents' urging, the opening of a bank account in my own name. Soon I was paying the Journal Company by check, and purchasing by check the operating essentials of an expanding business. I had to take some good-natured ribbing at the bank when adult depositors would step aside to permit a "big" depositor to get to the cashier window. After the novelty wore off, I stood in line like everyone else.

Peddling the paper wasn't too difficult once I learned at which door certain customers wanted their paper left and other individual idiosyncrasies. Techniques in by-passing yapping dogs were harder to learn. I never could determine whether some of those barking dogs were friendly or just interested in sinking their teeth into my leg.

Saturday was collection day. I kept a notebook with the names of all my customers and the amounts they owed. Even with the record I was sometimes questioned by customers who were delinquent in weekly payments. I soon learned not to permit a week to pass without collecting, if it were possible. It took a bit of strategy to cut short the conversations of talkative customers without being discourteous, but mostly I enjoyed the amiable chats with my regulars.

There was one place, though, that I approached with dread on collection day — the St. Paul railway depot. It was managed by one Ted Torkelson, who enoyed needling newsboys. Ted possessed hidden theatrical talents that Hollywood had overlooked. Of course, as a lad untutored in the ways of grownups, I didn't realize this but knew Ted only as a scary man with a thunderous voice. When it came time to collect from Ted, I solicited the services of my older brother, Joe, who had a paper route on the south end of town.

Ted was the busiest man in the world, or at least it seemed that way to me. Joe and I entered the station and Joe walked around the latticed divider that separated the waiting room from the inner sanctum that was Ted's office. Ted was hustling about, engaged in what to Joe and me was obviously some earth-shaking worldly problem, and Joe was loath to interrupt such a busy man. Joe stood patiently

149

at Ted's elbow. The soft whine of a distant train whistle was borne on east breezes. The telegraph clattered. Joe stood quietly, holding his breath. Ted ignored him. After what seemed an eternity, Ted turned and, feigning surprise at seeing Joe trembling at his elbow, demanded to know why he was standing there.

"I'm here to collect," Joe said.

"Collect for what?" Ted roared.

"For the *Journal*," Joe answered.

"What *Journal?*" Ted bellowed.

"Milwaukee Journal," Joe replied.

"How much is it?" Ted shouted.

"Twenty-eight cents, sir," Joe said.

"Oh," said Ted. "Why didn't you say so when you first came in? After this say what you're here for as soon as you come in. And say it LOUD. Here's the twenty-eight cents. Mark it paid."

These theatrics were varied only slightly by Ted on each collection day. Sometimes a faint chuckle could be heard following the incidents. But finally one Saturday Joe went to the depot, flung open the door, and shouted as loud as he could, *"JOURNAL* — TWENTY-EIGHT CENTS!"" Ted the Terror was stunned. Meekly, he handed over the twenty-eight cents. Victorious, Joe strode out jauntily. But Ted recovered quickly, and before the station door closed behind him, Joe heard Ted's booming voice barking, "MARK IT PAID!"

■■■

World's Greatest Cheesemaker

Sara Rath

Two elderly ladies stopped by my grandpa Kasper's cheese factory one day. While he filled their orders, one of the women asked, "How often do you make old cheese?" Without cracking a smile, Grandpa replied, "Every other day."

When P. H. Kasper wasn't busy making old cheese, he was busy making plain everyday cheddar cheese — seven days a week for more than fifty years — cheese that was famous throughout the world. His natural cheddar won more than two hundred awards, and he was proclaimed "World's Greatest Cheesemaker" at the 1912 International Dairy Show. In fact, Ripley's "Believe It or Not" column once claimed that P. H. Kasper had won more prizes than any other cheesemaker.

Grandpa Kasper made his first cheese at the age of seventeen. In 1891 he opened his own factory near Bear Creek. In 1893 he was awarded his first gold medal and diploma at Chicago's Columbian Exposition. Five years later he won the highest award at the Wisconsin State Fair, and in 1900 he won the Grand Prix at the Paris International Exposition. From then on he won nearly all the competitions he entered: The Pan American Exposition of 1901; the St. Louis Exposition of 1904; the National and International Dairy Shows of 1912; the Syracuse National Dairy Show in 1923; the Iowa Cattle Exposition in 1925 and 1926; and the Pacific Slope Fair in 1927. He won even though he was usually docked a point or two in competition due to the natural creamy color of his cheese — he seldom added artificial orange coloring.

P. H. Kasper was appointed by President Coolidge as a delegate to the International Dairy Conference in England in 1928. "It was the best time I ever had in my life," he recalled. After meeting King George V, he went on to Europe, where he spent months visiting other cheese factories and studying cheesemaking techniques.

The key to Grandfather's success as a cheesemaker probably came from his patience. He claimed that he made prize-winning cheese every day and, in fact, once pulled a cheese at random from the racks in the curing room. It won the highest rating ever given to a cheese. "To make good cheese," he said, "you must stay with it, live with it from the milk can to the curing rack. Many young men nowadays are in

151

too much of a hurry. I tell you, you can't make cheese in the morning and go to the ball game in the afternoon!''

In 1917, P. H. Kasper became one of the first cheesemakers to take orders for Christmas gift packages of cheese. One such package was a present from Governor William D. Hoard to a University of Chicago professor. The practice caught on, and by 1940 Grandpa was mailing out as many as 1,100 four-pound packages over the holiday season.

Of course, my grandfather usually had a hired man to help in the cheese factory, but Grandma Kasper and their eight children — Charlotte, Linda, Cecelia, Lester, Norma, Myrene, Margaret (my mother), and Lawrence — all shared certain responsibilities.

"Our job was to wash the separator plates," Myrene recalls. "The separator had fifty-two cones, and every day, after lunch, Margaret and I had to go down to the factory and scrub them with a scrub brush." The girls were also called on to clean the whey tank, sometimes going in barefoot to brush, rinse, and drain it.

"It took as long to make that factory clean as it did to make the cheese," Margaret says. "Because after the cheese was made, the floor was scrubbed. And I mean *scrubbed*. Every day."

"And then he had all the brass valves on the pipes polished," Myrene says. "One of the hired men had to polish all those valves. Everything always smelled clean. Even the windows were spotless."

The cheese factory and the big house on the hill above it were host to a steady stream of visitors. Grandpa Kasper seldom had time to sit down and rest, even on Sundays. "Dad would come up to the house," Myrene remembers, "and soon a car would drive in. Dad would look out. 'Somebody for cheese.' So he'd get up and go down to the factory to wait on customers. He'd usually bring them up to the house to show them the medals, and then they'd sit and talk."

"He went down to the university at Madison to teach," Margaret adds, "and a couple years he brought men home who'd taken his cheesemaking course. They'd say, 'Mr. Kasper, can I come home with you and learn some more?' He did that quite a few times."

"The hired men stayed with us, too," Myrene says, "and Mother would do their laundry and cook their meals. They'd have a room of their own. Those hired men were treated like part of the family. One hired man loved curd. He would put curd in his pockets, and Mother would go to wash his clothes and find a handful of curd in his pants."

Grandpa Kasper learned a technique in Europe that he applied to his own cheese factory. Grandpa dug a hole in front of the house, about fifteen feet deep, and from there dug a tunnel to the factory curing room, which was eighty or a hundred feet away. The tunnel surfaced

152

in the curing room, where there was an exhaust fan in the ceiling. On top of the hole in the front yard he placed a tower with a hornlike contraption his family called a wind catcher. It funneled air underground to the curing room and cooled the cheese. It was a primitive method of refrigeration, but it worked.

On the weekends, the Kasper children and their families gathered at home for dinner. My father and his brothers-in-law would grab an apron and help out in the factory. It was just a family thing to do, but Grandpa was always proud of their interest in his cheese. He was ill when I was born but lived to continue his work for another year or so.

In May of 1941, P. H. Kasper was recognized by the Wisconsin legislature for his fifty years of cheesemaking and his award-winning cheese. After his death, in December of 1942, Uncle Lester took over the factory. Grandma Kasper lived many more years in the house above the factory, and some of my happiest afternoons were spent there, looking at Grandpa's medals and trophies, listening to Sir Harry Lauder records on the windup Victrola in the parlor, looking at stereo views through a stereoscope. It was a place where I could sneak yet another piece of Grandma's famous thick-cream coffee cake (hidden in the second drawer from the top in the middle section of her kitchen cupboard) or curl up in the porch swing with a handful of warm curd.

Actually, as to which was the bigger attraction, it was probably a tie between the coffee cake and the curd. I remember waiting patiently beside the vat inside the factory for that magical moment when the curd would form. My mouth waters even now to recall the tender squeak of the curds against my teeth, and the warm, milky, heavenly flavor. Sometimes I'd be allowed inside the cool darkness of the curing room, where cheese was stacked high along the shelves in round wooden boxes. Uncle Lester would always ask if I wanted a sample. A taste, to Uncle Lester, meant a quarter-pound slab.

Uncle Lester died in 1971, my cousins chose other vocations, and the factory is closed and empty now. It was recently added to the National Register of Historic Places because of Phillip Kasper's fame. I'm glad Grandpa Kasper's cheese factory will be preserved, but the recognition doesn't make that little spot on the map any more special than it ever was — to me or to him.

"Was in the factory yesterday — it seemed good," he wrote to my mother shortly before his death. "They tell me I've made enough cheese, but what else should I do? I keep thinking about the cheese and all the things I've done with cheese, and now I've begun to get some ideas on how to make it better. I think I'll make the best cheese yet this summer...."

■■■

153

The Berry Pickers

Edith E. Fleming

In the spring of 1917, when I was 7½, our family moved from Middleton to Kennedy, where Dad had purchased forty acres of cutover land. In our first summer there we were introduced to wild berry picking. The berry season began after the Fourth of July and lasted into September. The Hank Calkins family took us on our first trips to the berry patches, which were abundant in the swamps and slashings of this logged-over land.

When we went berry picking, we wore long-sleeved shirts, straw hats, neckerchiefs, old shoes, and bib overalls. Our equipment was hardly sophisticated: syrup and lard pails in two-quart and gallon sizes (cleaned and saved against picking time), which we hung from the strap of our overalls, and a stick of chewing gum. The gum served two purposes: it kept our mouths moist and our berries in our pails.

The first of the bounty to supplement our winter's fare were wild strawberries, which we found along the railroad tracks and in old clearings where we knelt to pick the tiny sweet-tart fruits. We came home with pink knees, full pails, and big appetites. Then Ma would make her good short biscuits. The hot biscuits were split and heaped with

154

crushed, sweetened berries and rich canned milk was poured over all — I can taste it now!

In the slashings where the hot sun shone were red raspberries. After a summer shower, the steam rising from the berries smelled sweet. The best and biggest berries ripened where old stumps and logs lay. Perched on a log, you could fill your pail fast, but you had to be careful to keep your balance. Falling off a log didn't hurt; the resilient bushes cushioned you. What hurt was seeing the red juicy berries crushed among the canes. In a raspberry patch you "walked light." Jiggling or thumping your pail made a juicy mess of the delicate berries. It also made "picking over" difficult. Picking over was removing leaves, twigs, hulls, stinkbugs, green berries and various worms that ended up in your pail along with the berries. If a picking pail contained more than a handful of trash, you were considered a "dirty" picker who "brought home half the patch." You also picked over your own pail.

In the raspberry patches we listened for bees and bears. Yellow jackets built their nests on the ground and in rotting logs, and if you stepped on their "house" they defended it fiercely. Whenever that happened we dug frantically through the humus to reach clay, which we moistened with tea or water and pasted on the reddening stings. The little pats of wet clay and a rest in the shade gave some relief. None of us was ever chased from a berry patch by a bear. In fact, if a bear heard us coming, we heard him leave the patch. Whenever there were any bear signs in a patch, we stayed within sight and sound of one another, talking loudly, laughing and singing songs.

The best raspberries were in the Camp Two area. There was a clear, cool pool there. A stake near the pool held a tin drinking cup, and I always wondered who drank the sweet water before me. Another larger patch was quite a hike from home. We took the old right-of-way to the Camp Fifteen clearing and on to the "kickback." We passed Lake Annie where there was an abandoned boom floating low in the water. It was tempting to try to tiptoe along the boom, but only if someone older was with you.

Dewberries grew along the Omaha track, near the ruins of a roundhouse. We bent to pick these black beady berries from barbed vines. Good for jam, pies and eating "out of hand." But when blueberries were ripe, that was my favorite time. Every morning, when the dew was heavy on the tall swamp grass, Ma, Dad and I took a sandwich and a jar of tea apiece and our pails and hit the right-of-way to Camp One, then east on an old tote road to Round Lake. The mossy bog that surrounded this lake was where the dusted blue orbs grew, the blueberry bog. After the sun had dried my dew-wet clothes and the air hung hot and humid, I would find a knoll where I could fill my pail, and then poke my bare feet down through the moss into the black cold water beneath.

When we heard the two o'clock passenger train for Kennedy, we took our full pails and hit for home. My picking pail stayed on the bib strap of my overalls. Ma carried two water pailfuls; Dad carried two water pails and a pack sack with a fifty-pound lard can full. He put a board between the sharp can edge and his back so it wouldn't cut into his back.

These seemed like long days to a small girl and I was happy to come home to a warm meal, which my sisters had ready. They also had jars, rubber rings and lids clean and ready to fill. We picked over the berries on a newspaper-covered table as soon as we finished eating. Dad filled crates to sell to the train crews, who bought all we could spare. We took pride in selling the biggest, cleanest berries to them. Often on those warm summer nights, long after I had gone to bed, I awoke to the sounds of jars clinking and the soft murmur of my parents' voices. "You can tighten down the lids on those now, Ed." "That makes 26 quarts we have." The house smelled sweet and I often think of how hard they worked, gathering and preserving the berries, and of the pride they felt in counting the hot, full jars.

Gooseberries came somewhere in between dewberries and blueberries. They were prickly fruit to gather. I can still picture my dad the time when he slipped down a slanting log, lying with his berries spilled inside his jacket, unable to roll over, the prickly berries there. We had a good laugh after we scooped the berries back into his pail and found there were no broken bones. Ma tried removing the spines so she could make jam and pie, but the "grief outweighed the good" and the gooseberries were boiled, squeezed through a flour sack and made into a pale pink jelly. It was tart and tasted fine with roasted venison ribs.

After the first frost, the grownups went to the cranberry marsh west of Kennedy for a picnic lunch and to gather "mossberries." They'd come home with tubs and barrels of the firm glossy fruit. Sorting over those berries was a pleasure. All sizes, shapes and colors went into making the jars of sauce. The cranberries were usually canned in winter, when Ma had enough empty jars and plenty of sugar.

My sister, Lillian, knew of a secret spot where there were wintergreen berries, along the brushy edge of the "little swamp." We filled our lunch buckets on the way home from school. We sent small boxes of the red firm berries back to Middleton so friends and family there could delight in the delicate flavor of these berries. For a stronger flavor, you could chew the glossy, leathery leaves.

There were other fruits free for the picking too — wild cherries; choke, pin and black cherries, which made a rich syrup, or sometimes

Ma combined their juice with apple juice for a jelly that was as delicious to the taste as it was beautiful to look at in the glass jars. There was highbush cranberry, with its own distinct flavor. Thorn apples, which grew along Pine Creek, tasted bitter, and there were Juneberries near Pine Creek too. From this wild, cold land God gave us fruit for the gathering.

■■■

Home-Town Boom

Margaret I. Shale

By the turn of the century, North Freedom was practically a self-sustaining village of 500-600 people. Contributing to its lifeblood was the railroad. The Chicago & North Western passenger trains made eight stops a day. It was before the age of the auto when people began commuting to nearby cities to work, so the people who lived in North Freedom also worked in North Freedom. In addition to a sawmill, a blacksmith shop, and two grocery stores, there was a lumberyard, two warehouses where farmers waited in line in the fall to unload potatoes, a farm-implement shop, a barber shop, and a furniture store.

As a little girl of five or six, I enjoyed riding along with my parents in the buggy to get groceries, or take a can of cream to the creamery down by the river, where I could watch the big churn turn the cream to butter. I also liked to stop at Shug Elliot's candy store. He gave the biggest sackful of candy in town for a nickel. He would balance himself on one crutch and scoop wintergreen candies out of a big glass jar until the sack was filled with the aromatic pink candies with the XXX's on top! We always stopped at George Hackett's meat market too. A ring of his juicy homemade bologna was only a dime. I'd wave at Mr. Trumbul, in his open buggy, driving his team of prancing brown horses through town. Mrs. Trumbul ran a hotel across the street from the Methodist church. Opposite the church was the doctor's office. Dr. Whetmore, besides nursing me through pneumonia, pulled my first loose tooth.

It was during this time (about the year 1900) that North Freedom began to buzz with excitement. The Illinois Company, after taking a sample core, decided there was enough iron ore in the ground to pay the company to sink a shaft. They began hiring and miners came from as far away as Michigan. Rows of cottages for the miners were built up the road from the mine. The mining company also erected a big building to house the machinery and a dry-house with two long tanks where the men came to wash off the red mud from their hands and faces after coming out of the mine, and remove the oilcloth suits and high rubber boots they wore in the wet mine.

When the mine was in full operation, carloads of ore were shipped out on a spur track to the Chicago & North Western Railroad in North Freedom. A huge engine with two enormous flywheels hummed night and day as it ran the generator that created the electricity for lights and for the power to operate the wench that hauled up the ore. There were also five or six boilers in the engine house. The steam from these boilers fueled the big pumps that kept the mine from flooding. A constant stream of red water ran from the mine into Seely Creek, which wound through the mining village of LaRue. On hot summer days school boys would strip and jump into the red water, plaster themselves with red mud, then sit on the bank to let it dry, and pretend they were Indians.

School boys weren't the only thing that was red. Red paint was made from the ore, so the railroad company used it to paint their boxcars and farmers used it to paint their barns. Waste ore was used as road material, and the road from LaRue to North Freedom was "barn red" for years.

The men were carried down into the mine and up again in the same buckets used for bringing out the ore. But my father-in-law steadfastly refused to ride up in the skips, always climbing the long, slippery ladder instead. He feared that the wrong signal might be given and they would be hauled to the top of the tipple, forty or fifty feet up, and dumped into the ore cars. (It finally did happen once, causing one man's death.) In the mine, mules pulled trams along the passageways, called drifts. The drifts, shored up by heavy timbers, led out in different directions and on different levels from the main shaft.

Before long, the little village of LaRue was prospering. There was a hotel (where, on Sunday, they served big dishes of homemade ice cream and crackers for a dime), a lumberyard, a grocery store, two taverns, a blacksmith shop and a church. In turn, North Freedom began to boom too. Another doctor came to town, and prescriptions could be filled at the new drug store. Myrtle Corb opened a millinery shop and there was a dentist office over the bank.

A second mine, the Iroquois, began operating and shortly thereafter more businesses came. A hardware store opened, then a general store, owned by A.A. Johnson, who gave out calendar plates at Christmas. Lange and Eschenbach opened another grocery store. Mrs. Trumbul had more patrons than she could accommodate, so a second hotel was built. Will Schmidt established a livery stable across the street from the Trumbul Hotel.

Then, almost as quickly as it began, the boom ended. It became more and more expensive to mine the ore, and finally both mines were abandoned and the entrances sealed. The miners left and the cottages were sold. Slowly the little town of LaRue faded away. The store, hotel, and church were closed. North Freedom was also affected. Dentists, doctors, lumberyards, newspaper office, meat markets, creamery — all closed their doors. Today only a bank, post office, one grocery store and three churches remain of the original boom town.

■ ■ ■

The Guardian

Charlotte Goshorn

I grew up on the Wisconsin shore of Lake Superior in an old house whose timbers had become uniquely attuned to the gales that blew across the lake. All the interior doors of the house would slam shut to signal the imminent arrival of a storm. Although we couldn't see the water from the house, the direction and force of the wind made the poplar leaves rustle in a certain way, and the sky took on a distinctive gray color. Soon the measured roar of crashing waves would reach our ears.

Afterward, my brother and sister and I would run the five hundred yards to the lake, eager to see what surprises the storm might have left on the narrow strip of beach that formed the north border of our farm. We ran in the order of our ages: eleven-year-old Gene first; I, nine years old, close behind; and, struggling to keep up, seven-year-old Marian. We slowed our pace at the wooden bridge spanning the slough. Home of pond lilies and dragonflies, the quiet water surpported a split-level ballet of water striders and sunfish that fascinated us. From the bridge, a short walk over a hummock of sand bordered by coarse grass brought us to the lakeshore.

Sometimes we found the beach widened and cluttered with shining chips of shells, new pebbles, and driftwood. At other times the sand was littered with the flotsam of a thousand islands and as many ships. We never found anything valuable, but we were nevertheless intrigued by the assortment of containers, sodden bits of clothing, and shattered boards.

One summer evening, while we stood in the gathering darkness and gazed at the aftermath of a gale, Marian and I found a small brass fitting attached to a fine-grained piece of wood. We wondered if it had broken loose from one of the iron-ore carriers whose lights we could see on the far horizon. Gene insisted it must have come from a fancy yacht anchored off the Apostle Islands. On the way home, he told us stories of shipwrecks and drownings. Then, in a lowered voice, he said that *ghosts* lingered where ships went down.

Hearing this, Marian and I ran to the house, barricaded ourselves in our bedroom, and listened tensely as Gene slowly ascended the stairs,

161

making "ghost" noises all the while, entered his adjoining room, and tapped on our wall. We shrieked in delighted terror.

The next day was Sunday, so we were free to explore the lakefront all afternoon. The water was still choppy. The surf had dug deeply into the pebbled wave-line and pushed the sand into an unusually steep bank. Carrying our shoes, we slogged through the loose sand, taking care to avoid the cold water of Lake Superior. We looked for the valuable rocks and minerals Gene believed might someday be there for us to find, picking up stones and dropping them, inspecting what barnacle shells there were, and studying the smooth patina of waterworn sticks. A few shorebirds, preoccupied in their own kind of treasure hunt, alighted near us. We talked little, slowly making our way about a mile up the beach.

Late in the afternoon we came upon a phenomenon we had never before encountered. A stream known as Fish Creek had been completely dammed up by the recent storm. A mound of wet sand lay across the mouth of the creek, and a large pool of dark water had accumulated behind this dam. Upstream, the span of an abandoned wooden bridge hung a few feet above the swollen creek.

Always before we had halted our explorations at the mouth of Fish Creek, partly because of its width, but mostly because of the gloomy atmosphere of the area. An old log house, collapsing from summer rot, was reflected in the slow water where the creek curved out of sight around a rank growth of trees. Long strands of algae waved from submerged logs. An unhealthy sheen on the stream's surface prevented a clear view of its depths.

At that moment, however, my thoughts were only of the beach beyond. I joyfully realized we could cross the creek on the sandbar and examine unfamiliar territory before it was time to return home. I started toward the wet sand, but my brother caught my arm and stopped me. He stood there for a moment, studying the scene.

"It might be quicksand," he said. "We'd better not cross it."

I accepted his assessment of the danger because he took seriously his responsibility for our safety. Still, the idea of exploring on the other side of the creek appealed to me very strongly. I called upon Gene to find a way.

"Easy," he said, "if that old bridge will hold our weight."

We struck off through a tangle of bushes and trees to look at the bridge. As we pushed the undergrowth out of our way, Gene asked, "Did I ever tell you this bridge is haunted, and so is that cabin over there?"

To bolster my courage, I challenged him. "How can a bridge be haunted when nobody ever lived on it?"

"Old Jim Mutch told Dad and me about it once," he continued.

"A French trapper who lived in that cabin fell from the bridge and drowned. His wife never gave up looking for his body, even after she died of old age."

"How did anybody know who they were? You told us ghosts were pale and you could see right through them," I argued stoutly.

"Some, yes," Gene admitted. "But ghosts take different shapes. Some like to be so thin you can hardly see them, and others like to be all dressed up in fancy clothes."

The thought of clothed ectoplasm, indistinguishable from living persons, dampened my bravado considerably. Marian had hurried ahead of me, so now I walked last in line. I kept looking over my shoulder, nervous about movements in the bushes behind me.

We broke out of the woods just then and approached the bridge. Gene pointed out some loose planking and missing boards. If there ever had been a guardrail along the sides, it had long since tumbled into the stream. The water was lapping high on the pilings. To make matters worse, none of us could swim. I lost all eagerness to cross over, but Gene must have felt a challenge to try the aging bridge.

He made his way out onto it, testing it with his weight at each step. Then he arrived at the perfect logic to convince us — and himself — that the bridge must be safe. "If it held up this well when the ice went out last spring, it must be pretty strong," he said.

Marian and I followed him onto the weathered planks. The bridge swayed a little. We hardly noticed the cloud shadows that passed over us. Slowly, carefully, we inched our way across, not daring to look down at the murky water. There was one particularly bad place. Here, a single twelve-inch plank led from one piling to another. As we crossed, we held hands and joked half-heartedly about knowing how it felt to "walk the plank." My knees shook. The loose boards rattled and Marian clung to my dress as we made our way to the far side.

The alder swamp bordering the creek on this side looked forbidding. The trees had a dank white mold on their stunted branches, and even the spiders we saw were fat and white. We kept to the highest ground, stepping on tussocks of spongy moss to avoid the pools of water that were gathering from the backed-up stream. Almost at the edge of the swamp, Gene stopped short. Blocking our path, a hornets' nest hung from a low branch.

"We'll have to run for it," Gene said.

"Can Marian run fast enough?" I wondered aloud.

"We'll take hold of her and pull her along with us," Gene answered.

I wasn't sure we could run fast enough dragging Marian, but I knew we all had to pass under the branch together. The hornets, once aroused by our nearness, would begin an angry pursuit without delay. Gene took a firm grip on Marian's right arm; I took her left. On the count of three, we rushed out of the swamp to the buzzing of a swarm of insects. An offshore wind slowed their speed enough to allow our escape unscathed.

We made our way back out to the beach. There, we noted that the sky had filled with gray clouds, the wind was picking up, and the lake was getting choppy. No time remained to do more exploring. A storm was brewing, and we had to find a way to get home quickly.

Gene tested the firmness of the sandbar across Fish Creek. His footprint grew ominously deeper and filled with water. He looked toward the bridge, but that route was cut off by the hornets. The waves were pounding harder now. As we watched, countless pebbles were pulled under water by the fierece undertow.

"We've got to dig a channel so the creek can flow out to the lake again," Gene announced. "We'll be able to see how deep the water is, and then we can wade across." His decision was based on limited knowledge and a lot of boyish daring.

The three of us got on our knees and dug in the wet sand with our fingers. The shallow trench we made filled almost instantly with a trickle of water from the dammed-up creek. The trickle quickly expanded to a small stream. As the force of the rushing water scoured away the sand dam and carried it out into the lake, the channel widened rapidly and churned down to its original stony bed. The banks of the sandbar caved in. The mouth of the creek widened to three feet, four feet. We stood back and watched the power of the water swirling toward the freedom of the lake. In minutes, the width of the outlet had grown to six feet, ten feet. I think it was then that Gene realized that the force of the water increased with every foot of width it gained.

"We'd better get across," he shouted, catching Marian's hand. She whimpered and held back so fearfully that he had to pick her up and carry her across. At midstream he yelled something, but the noise of the water and waves drowned out his words. The water curled wildly around his legs until he stepped out on the other side. He turned to call to me. The creek was twelve feet across now. I looked longingly at the bridge, shrouded in lowering mists, then turned my face into the wind for a last look at the scudding spray over the lake. A brown streak of sandy water colored the waves out to a distance of some fifty feet. I saw my brother turn away, pushing my sister ahead of him as if to start for home. An overwhelming sense of abandonment swept over me. The thought of being left alone on the lakeshore during the storm, especially in this dreary place, was unbearable.

I plunged over the crumbling sandbank and into the rushing water. I felt a strong tugging at my legs. Dark ripples splashed against my hips, and I could feel a tumble of gravel rolling over my feet. With every step I nearly lost my footing, and I wondered if I could make

164

my way more firmly on hands and knees.

As I bent over, I heard my brother's voice and looked up. He was standing at the edge of the channel, facing me, his hands cupped around his mouth. I could not make out what he was saying, so I tried to draw closer. With each step I took, my feet slid sideways over the pebbles and I was pulled closer to the lake. My eyes were riveted on the tense face of my brother. He threw himself outstretched on the crumbling sand, reaching toward me with one arm and gesturing wildly with the other. I looked upstream to where he was pointing.

I do not know how many seconds I remained there, rooted against the mad power of the stream. There are times, during moments of crisis, when the mind speeds up and the imagination breaks free of time and logic. As I gazed toward the far place between the murky water and heavy mist, the bridge appeared to have railings of new brown lumber; the planks shone sturdy and bright in a shaft of sunlight. Drawn by four horses and guided by a capped driver, a covered carriage with brass fittings emerged from the woods at the landing. As the horses' hooves made an echoing staccato sound on the fresh planks, I could see the occupant of the coach, a handsome red-haired woman in dark clothing. She turned toward me and looked directly into my eyes.

Then, to my horror, one of the horses stumbled and broke through the railing. In an accelerating disaster, the remaining horses, coach, driver, and lady were dragged over the side and disappeared into the opaque water. In the next instant, my eyes focused on something bearing down on me. It was a huge span of the bridge, at least twenty feet wide, which had been torn loose in the swirling current and was now being borne toward the outlet where I stood.

I must have screamed. I tried to make a jump for my brother's outstretched hand, but the channel had widened further and put him out of reach. I lost my footing and fell gasping into the warm, sandy water. My body rolled quickly to the swiftest portion of the stream. I felt myself sink lower and lower until my shoulders and knees scraped against the rough pebbles of the streambed. Suddenly I found myself atop a grating mound of wet stones. Gene took hold of my arms and pulled me out of the channel onto dry sand.

I lay there for a time, choking and weeping, coming to myself and the present moment. Gene pounded my shoulders, and Marian came close and cried in sympathy.

Finally I sat up and pieced together what must have happened. Just as I fell into the stream, the span of bridge had slammed across the outlet, blocking the creek. This had made it possible for Gene to jump into the greatly diminished flow and drag me to safety. Even as I sat there, the force of the water was undermining the section of

165

the planks and gaining new momentum.

Abrasions from the stony creek-bed began to smart along my legs and arms. We stood up. "You saved my life," I said to Gene.

"I think that helped," he said, pointing to the dam of boards. "And" — he paused — "maybe the ghost of the bridge is a guardian of some kind."

I could not answer. I did not want to confess what I had seen for fear he would ridicule my wild imagination. But I wondered if he had seen the redhaired woman too. Had we both glimpsed the guardian? Or had the ghostly vision been merely a distortion of the bridge and the wind-whipped trees behind it? Still unable to think clearly, I felt stunned and exhilarated at the same time.

A roll of thunder awakened us to the realization that we faced a two-mile walk to reach shelter. As we took Marian's hands and started for home, she asked, "What's a guardian?"

Gene and I looked at each other. Without exchanging a word, we decided never to tell our parents the full story of the day's events. And to keep Marian from telling them, we answered her question with a long and involved explanation. We wanted to close her mind on all remembrance of this afternoon, much as the north wind closed the doors of our house before a storm.

And we never spoke of the guardian again.

■ ■ ■

Bull Cooks and Road Monkeys

Samuel H. Thut

W riters of historical lumberjack lore have neglected them, giving preference to their more flamboyant co-workers. They were usually considered the lowest category of workers in the lumberjack trade. Yet bull cooks and road monkeys had more to do with horses than anyone else except the teamsters, and there was a time from the late 1800s to about 1930 when horses were the only means of power to move timber from the forest to river, railroad or mill. Horses were accorded almost equal consideration in shelter, feeding and care as the men. In fact, there were times when some men felt the horses had priority.

In early logging days job descriptions were simple and above all truthful. ''Bull cook'' is a combination of bull, another word for ox, and cook, a title applied to a man who worked around camp and fed something or someone. Literally, a bull cook was a feeder of oxen. Even with the later predominance of horses he was still known as the bull cook. His job also included a multitude of other tasks unrelated to the care of animals.

His chores started early in the morning before anyone else was up. He started or stoked up the fires in every building in camp, then at 4:30 a.m. he woke up the teamsters in the teamster's shanty, lit their lanterns and pumped water for their horses. The teamsters meanwhile fed, watered, curried and brushed and harnessed their teams. Teamsters, or "skinners," were rated and paid by the number of horses they drove, so that a four-horse teamster was a top pay man followed by the regular single-team and the one-horse skinner who only took care of one horse.

At 5:30 the bull cook lit all the lamps in the other bunkhouses. At that time the cook or "cookee" would blow the camp horn, a four-foot-long sheet-metal instrument with a flared bell and a standard cornet mouthpiece. "You've gotta getup, you've gotta getup," could be heard for miles in the cold winter morning air.

The second horn at 6:00 a.m. was a call to breakfast. After breakfast when the teams were all out and the day beginning to break the bull cook cleaned the barns. After the barn work was done, he used a sturdy hand sled to haul a day's supply of wood to the bunkhouses, cook shanty and "wanigan." Wood for the cook stove had to be finely split hardwood with some dry pine "rampike" wood for kindling to get the stove hot in the morning for frying pancakes.

Water for the camp buildings he pumped or drew from a well and carried in two 16-quart galvanized pails on a yoke to fill the water barrels in the cook shanty. One of the barrels served as a reservoir to the cookstove and furnished an abundance of hot water. There were cold-water barrels in each of the bunkhouses and a twenty-five pound metal lard container on the heating stove for hot water for wash up. A large galvanized pail with a dipper for drinking water stood next to the wash-up sink. Towels were hung on rollers nearby which the bull cook washed and changed each day.

Cleaning the "rampastures" — the bunkhouses — was another one of his duties. He swept them but never had to pick up any dirt because it all fell between the cracks in the floor boards. Floors were mopped and broom scrubbed every couple of weeks, weather permitting. Then there were the lamp chimneys to be cleaned as well as the globes for each teamster's lantern, and the lanterns had to be kept filled with kerosene.

During the day all the camp heaters had to be kept burning too, but having started his day before anyone else, the bull cook usually had several hours to rest during the afternoon. It was a servantlike job, seven days a week, paid by the month. One small reward was that he did not have to clean the barns on Sunday. The teamsters did it because on that day they did not work the horses.

Along with all his work he had some authority, assigning bunks to new men, stalls to teams coming in, and guarding everything around

168

the camp during the day. This guardianship extended to watching camp during the intervals between the main logging operations, often with only a dog for companionship.

"Road monkeys" were sometimes called chickadees because they had one thing in common with the little birds: horse manure. Chickadees, the birds, lived along the haul roads and thrived on undigested oats which they picked from horse manure. The road monkey's job was to remove the manure from the iced haul roads because even a small amount of it had a braking effect under the runners of a sleigh with a heavy load. So when a teamster said chickadee it could mean either a bird or a man.

When the first teamster went into the woods to haul a sleigh load of logs, the road monkey rode with him. His most important duty was at the "ramdowns." These were places on the haul roads where the steep downhill grade was a hazard to both team and teamster. Once out of control a load of logs could be a killer. Breaking the speed and momentum of a load whose weight was many, many times greater than the weight of the horses was accomplished by putting hay or sand in the sleigh runner tracks, or ruts. To be effective and create friction these materials had to be reasonably dry, and free from frost, ice or snow. Upon reaching the "hay hill" the road monkey would shake up the hay to get the frost and snow out of it. He'd add a little more hay in the tracks where it was worn thin or lost and then wait for the first load to come along. If the hill was very long or steep a good teamster would stop at the top, walk down and check conditions, maybe add a little hay or take away some. It was easy to get hung up on the hill where intervals of hay were too long, though most teamsters preferred to have their teams do some pulling on the way down. When the first load had passed, the road monkey would have a pretty good idea as to how other loads and other teamsters would perform. The best road monkeys were former teamsters, men who were no longer able, either because of age or injuries, to drive or manage a four-horse team. After the hills were taken care of, horse manure removal was his main work for which he used a light long-handled shovel. He also carried an ax to cut a new rut or groove where a sleigh runner was jumping the track or cut skids to raise a runner above a rock that could cause a heavy load to become stuck.

Generally speaking, bull cooks and road monkeys were old lumberjacks, single men without nearby relatives who had spent a lifetime working in the woods. In most instances their glory days were past. Their menial employment was a source of security in their declining days and years, and it provided them an opportunity to continue living in the surroundings to which they had been long accustomed. Their employers usually had a degree of charitableness toward them and often

169

cared for them even after they could no longer perform the most menial tasks.

For them, Social Security came too late.

■ ■ ■

Milwaukee County Hospital 1925

Laura M. Hansen

I t was a beautiful day in September 1925. I got off the street-car at the end of the line in Wauwatosa. Recently widowed and in my twenties, I was entering Milwaukee County Hospital School of Nursing. I had already completed one and a half years of training at a La Crosse hospital. I entered a very old building that resembled an ancient castle and proceeded down a spacious, heavily tiled hall to the nurses' office, where the supervisor assigned me a room in the nurses' home. Three of us shared the room, which had two dressers, two closets and two beds, with a third bed on a sleeping porch.

House rules were very strict. We had to be in our rooms with lights out by ten p.m. and were allowed one late leave a week until twelve. I was given board, room, laundry and books without charge. There was no complaint regarding the amount of laundry sent in, but if a nurse appeared slovenly on duty, she was sent from the floor. Weekdays we worked from 7 to 7 with two hours off; on Sundays we worked half a day. In the evening we attended classes at the Milwaukee Vocational School. First-year students received five dollars per month, second-year students ten dollars, and third-year students earned fifteen dollars a month salary. My uniform was a grey and white striped one-piece dress with stiffly starched white collar, bib and full apron, and black stockings and oxfords.

The hospital had four main divisions: the men's Medical and Surgical and the women's Medical and Surgical. In each division there were three long adjoining wards with about twenty beds in each ward. There were many dimly lit tunnels under the hospital. One led to the Nurses' Home, another led to the morgue. If a female patient died, I had to escort her body to the morgue through the long, narrow tunnel.

My first assignment was to the men's Surgical Ward. At night there was only one student nurse and an intern for the fifty male pa-tients. The men seemed contented in their clean beds and were in-structed by the doctors to obey the nurses or they would have to leave. The lights, except for the desk light at the nurses' station, were turned off at 10 p.m., so when I worked the night shift I carried a kerosene lantern as I completed my chores. Moving from bed to bed in those dimly lit wards, I felt a kinship with Florence Nightingale.

One noon I was assigned the task of serving the meal. I knew what to serve each patient, but how to do it alone was a problem. Before the floor nurse left for the day, she picked out a 14-year-old Negro patient, Sammy, to help me. Sammy donned a chef's cap and apron and walked proudly beside me as I moved through the wards with the food cart filled with dishes and trays of steaming hot food. There was quite a variety of food for the many special diets, but one item that was never served was pork chops. The patients, including Sammy, knew this. Sammy, however, wanted to be entertaining, so as we moved along he called out, "Poke chops today! Poke chops!" The patients all smiled.

Most of the patients were well-behaved and rarely gave us any trouble. There were instances, though, like the night a patient suffering from delirium tremens caused a commotion. I was called to the lower ward by another patient, and as I neared the bathroom door a huge, six-foot raging hulk came toward me, shouting "Look out or I'll choke you!" My five-foot-two frame froze in place. Then he said, "They're after me, they're after me!" I quickly replied, "They are? I'll go see." And believe me I went — to the telephone. The night supervisor and an intern soon got him under control.

My operating room training was somewhat of a fiasco. As a flunky, I picked up and counted the bloody gauze sponges the surgeons sometimes threw about. That wasn't so bad but once, when I was scrub nurse, I nearly fainted and had to leave the room. In my rush to get out I cut through a back room and there lay a severed human leg still on the table. That didn't help matters any. Of course, there were lighter moments too, like the time in the operating room when all the nurses' eyes twinkled above their masks and there was an air of suppressed excitement. It seems the surgeon was losing his pants while operating. It was hard to keep from giggling. Finally a male orderly was called in and reached under the doctor's gown to tie the pants up so the doctor didn't have to contaminate his gloves and gown.

During the course of my training I served three months in the Milwaukee Children's Hospital and two weeks in the old Emergency Hospital downtown. Then I was chosen with three others to take the Public Health Course offered at the Wisconsin Anti-Tuberculosis Association, and for four months we accompanied the county and school nurses in their work and attended classes. I also accompanied the Visiting Nurses for one week. Toward the end of my schooling I worked the night shift on the women's Medical Ward. It was extremely discouraging and the hardest of all my training. After completing my evening chores, I donned a gown, mask, and rubber gloves and went

172

into the venereal nursery where many babies had gonorrhea-infected eyes. I washed the pus from their eyes with an eye dropper attached to a bottle of boric solution, then changed and fed them. It was a pitiful place and tears often came to my eyes when I heard them cry, seemingly unloved.

In February 1927 I wrote my State Board exam for RN. I applied for a position with the Rhinelander Visiting Nurses Association and was accepted in March 1927.

■■■

The Drawn Shade

Ann Honeyager Baumgard

R ight across the road from the farmhouse where I was raised, stood a huge brick house, the country home of a city banker. Just a stone's throw from the mansion was a little tenant house for a farmhand, as the banker did not farm the land himself. A tiny chicken house, a wood shed, and a little outhouse sheltered by lilacs made up the tenant's domain. A bit of land, perhaps an acre or two, provided space for a big garden with room enough left for a few chickens to roam.

For a while, the tenant house had stood empty. Then, early one spring, a middle-aged Swedish couple moved in, and brought with them a mystery: Why was the shade of one room always kept tightly drawn, while all the others were raised high to let in bright cheerful sunshine?

All of us kids who attended Lawrence School trudged along the gravel road and passed the house of mystery day after day. But none of us, not even the biggest and bravest eighth-grade boys had nerve to ask the lady — on those rare occasions when she was seen — and certainly no one was courageous enough to knock at the door! Once, when we saw the lady way back in the garden, two of the boldest crept up close to the house, hoping to get a peek through the crack below the drawn shade.

"What did you see? Did you hear anything? Was someone inside?" we all chorused as they dashed back to the road where we all stood expectantly and open-mouthed.

"Nothin'," was the reply. "Seen nothin', heard nothin'. Let's get out of here!"

Gravel flew under rushing feet until we were well away from the house of mystery.

"Someday we'll all go together and ask her when she's workin' out in back, and if she chases us, we can run like crazy!"

Unfortunately we were never lucky enough to see the lady outside again, so we speculated among ourselves. "Bet they're hiding a fugitive from the law; a relative, maybe," suggested Willie.

"Maybe they've got a kid who's too crazy to go to school and they keep him locked up," was Herbie's offering.

"I'll bet there's somebody in there who's real old or real sick, and it's kept dark so that person will think it's night and will sleep all the time," said Laura. She was sure because her grandma's room had been kept dark before she died.

My sister and I asked Ma and Pa about the mystery, but they only told us to mind our own business.

In the evening the four of us would sit on the back steps to watch the fireflies in the hayfield, or to listen to the frogs tuning up for their concerts down by the creek, or to swat those mosquitoes that dared to penetrate the clouds of smoke from Pa's pipe. It was then that we could see the silhouette, moving about, against the drawn shades of the tenant house across the road.

"Look," Pa said one night, "there's something goin' on across the road. Been goin' on too long. You kids are right. One of these days I just might mosey over and find out what's goin' on. Maybe we can help."

But on the Friday before Decoration Day, before Pa could carry out his threat, the mystery was solved. We were dismissed early that day from school, and as we approached the little tenant house, we were surprised to see the lady waiting for us.

"Come, children, I want to show you sometin'. Come. Come," she coaxed. The most daring went first and the rest of us slunk behind.

"Come. Gather round. Little ones by front," she said, as she led us into the mystery room.

She pulled the chain to a tiny electric bulb suspended from the ceiling. We all gawked around. There was no invalid in a bed, no fugitive, no strange child. All we could see was a very old incubator.

"Ever you see baby Guineas hatch? Wait, I pull out egg drawer from this hatchin' machine."

She did just that, and all of us stood and stared.

"Golly, gee!" whispered Henry.

"Holy smokes! Look!" gasped Vincent.

There was a chorus of aw's, oh's, and lookee's as all of us watched the mystery of life emerging from the eggs.

The drawer of the "hatchin' machine" stood open. One baby, apparently the first one hatched, was dry and fluffy, alternately dozing and teetering under the lights above the drawer. Another had just tumbled out of its shell, wet and seemingly helpless.

"That one's dying," whispered Ethel.

"No, he ain't. He's weak from getting out of his shell," soothed the lady.

The eggs were in different stages of hatching. Some babies were half out of their shells, and others had just their little beaks showing.

Some eggs just sat there! On each egg were four numbers, 1-2-3-4, spaced equally around the whole egg. "What are the numbers on the eggs for?" I asked.

"Each night I turn egg to a new number. Then each part of egg gets a special time right under light. So that way there will be no cripples. You see, a mama hen turns eggs too when she moves around on her nest."

"Why did you keep the shade down?" Lee asked. We hardly dared to breathe while she answered.

"Oh, to keep drafts out and sunshine, so heat always stay even. It's like we do in Sweden. Keep even temperature."

All of us stood entranced at the miracle of little chicks coming out of the eggs. Time flew by, and within the hour of careful watching all twenty-four eggs hatched, and before long, twenty-four dark gray, white-spotted fluffy babies peeped and dozed in the warmth.

"Them's chickens," said Mat, thinking of our chicks at home.

"No, these babies is Guinea hens. They're like watchdogs when they grow up. They squawk and screech at strange things. Keep chicken hawks away."

As she walked over to the window to pull up the shade, she said to us, "Now go tell your papas and mammas what you see. And come again soon to see how fast these little fellers grow."

And the shade was drawn no more.

■■■

Township Christmas

Justin Isherwood

C hristmas is the farmers' holiday. The reason is one of logistics. Memorial Day, Independence Day, and Labor Day all come at a time when farmers cannot take liberties with their vocation. That the rest of the nation celebrates makes little difference. Christmas, on the other hand, comes at a time when the fields lie frozen and resting from the marathon event of summer. Work has cooled its fevered pace; the mows, granaries, and warehouses attest to the green season's end.

It is a primitive heritage, this winter holiday. Sky watchers, who by nature were farmers, for millenia noted the autumnal declination of the sun. Because of their direct relationship with the earth, the shorter, colder days no doubt caused a recurring fear among those early agriculturists that the sun would sink altogether beneath the horizon, never to rise again.

Perhaps their celestial instrument was a tree seen from their habitation, perhaps a large rock. No matter. Two thirds of the way through December, the sun rose on the north side of that tree or rock and gave notice that its ascension and the connected growing season were assured.

Modern farmers are yet tied to ancient solar rites. The autumn rush of canning, pickling, and hunting is but preparation to endure the winter's worst, to survive to a distant spring. The winter solstice is a nearly universal time of celebration, feast days, dances, and gift giving. Its importance is held within our being as an almost genetic response to a titled planet's returning swing about a nearby star.

American Indian legends tell of winter as a starvation time, tell how some were reduced to cannibalism in order to survive. The custom of celebration and gift giving served to reinforce the bonds of family, so the clan or tribe would not succumb to the dark possibilities of winter.

Such primitive notions seem far removed from the advertised gentility of the present age, but the township still harbors such historic alliance of community. Here, the relationship of one generation to another is functional. So too is the giving of gifts.

Christmas is a time when, for a moment, we are all believers in magic. The selfish find themselves generous; the quiet find themselves singing. It is a time when people become a little crazy and take to hiding things in secret places. A time when country boys sneak to the barn on Christmas Eve and sit in the dark, waiting to hear cows speak in human tongues. A time when the weed pullers of summer walk their fields spreading thistle, sunflower, and rye seeds, hoping for a blessing flight of birds over their land in the belief that feathered prayers are best. A time when children leave a plate of cookies for the storied red-suited gentleman, an act uncharacteristic of sweet-toothed youngsters.

That the season is generous cannot be doubted. The cash register carols ring in the ears of the nation's GNP. But amid the multitude of store-shelf curiosities, we have lost something of self-expression, a quality now thought quaint. It is the gift of self that reinforces the bonds of friends and family, and repairs the rents made in the communal fabric. It speaks of goodness, of character.

Remembered are all the knitted socks, caps, and mittens that mothers forced habitually on their children, despite the children's best efforts to lose, mutilate, or outgrow them. Remembered, too, are the flannel pajamas and the quilts stuffed with raw wool or old wedding suits. They were warm comfort in wood-heated, sawdust-insulated houses. As surely as people made these gifts, these gifts made the people.

Indeed, there were store-bought BB guns, toy trains that puffed flour smoke, Raggedy Ann dolls, and bicycles. There were baseball bats, Flexible Flyers, and ice skates. But beyond the store-bought were other contraptions, inventions of glue and jack plane, of countersunk screw and dovetail mortise. In the lingering warmth of the loving hands that made them, these were gifts that conveyed affection.

178

There were dollhouses with tiny doors and itsy-bitsy cupboards, even two-holers out back. Bookshelves and basswood mixing spoons, breadboards and spice racks. A coffee table with a purple blemish, testifying to the fence staple some great-grandfather had driven into the tree from which the table came. A child's wagon, its white-ash wheels turned on a basement lathe; a cradle with birch headboard; a dulcimer of prized black walnut. And a rocking chair, made from pine, pegged and glued. In it were lulled to sleep three generations of babies; in it were rocked away the anxious days of two world wars and one jungle fight.

There were even simpler gifts. A pancake breakfast shared with neighbors; the sudden appearance of two cords of oak firewood; snow tires mysteriously installed. Notes in the bottom of stockings promised two Sunday mornings of skipping church or three choreless Saturday mornings to go romp in the woods. Some notes promised simply to reveal a favorite fishing hole or a tree where flickers nested.

There was a gift, too, in all the cookies cut and made in the shape of angels and stars and reindeer. To children, it was a gift of powerful pride that they might decorate stars from their humble perch behind the steamed-up windows of a country kitchen.

A township Christmas was homegrown popcorn, spotted kernels of red and purple and bright yellow, shelled on the living-room floor, cobs tossed to the fire. It was hazelnuts to crack — by kids sitting cross-legged near the stove. It was ice-skating on the irrigation pit, with popple-branch hockey sticks and stone pucks. It was hot cider, suet pudding, black fudge, cranberry bread, and oyster stew.

And it was the tree brought home from the woodlot in the emptied honey wagon. That great green tree swelled the whole house with its vapors, its fragrance and good cheer, leaving few lives untouched by a simple, if pagan, act.

Christmas in the township still takes its cue from that generous bounty first given by the land. It was in just such a country place that angels were heard to sing of a child laid in a feedbox. It was, as all farmers know, a good place to be born.

■■■

179

Through the Rapids of the Flambeau

Alonzo W. Pond

Y ou ought to go down the Flambeau if you want a canoe trip. There's where you get real canoeing, but you've got to have a guide who knows the rapids if you expect to come out alive.'' That remark heard some five years ago made the Flambeau the goal of my winter dreams.

A two hundred mile paddle up the Wisconsin River landed me at the portage into Tomahawk Lake in August, 1919. I paddled to Minocqua, then portaged by rail to Boulder Junction near the head waters of the Manitowish.

My equipment consisted of a fourteen foot canvas canoe, *Laura L,* a pup tent and a one man "go light" camping outfit.

The north fork of the Manitowish rises in the lakes of western Vilas County, Wisconsin, and after joining the Bear becomes the Flambeau.

Paddling alone is lonesome and I hurried over the first miles of the river in an effort to reach Park Falls, where I was to meet Dad, as quickly as possible. While spending a rainy day in a deserted hunter's cabin I had the good fortune to be joined by two lads from Detroit who were making the trip in an eighteen foot E.M. White canoe. We decided to stick together and the next morning set out to try our first rapids.

Below the mouth of the Turtle River we entered a stretch known as Seven Mile Rapids, in the first five miles of which there are twelve distinct rapids containing drops of from three to seven feet. It was my luck to go ahead on two of the worst pieces.

The first, Quins' Rapids, was a real thriller. At that point the shores are rocky and a few boulders have strayed out into the stream. The Waves! They looked to be five feet high to our inexperienced eyes and perhaps they were; at any rate my little *Laura L* didn't rise quite high enough on the first one and a good chunk of wave came aboard. The duffel kept the water from running back so that the added weight was all in the bow and when she hit the next wave she made no attempt to go over it; stuck her nose in and plowed straight through.

For the next few seconds my mind was far from dwelling on the beauties of nature and wholly occupied with the problem of keeping the temperamental *Laura L* and her load from going over. I finally reached shore and bailed out while I watched the long *Pardner* leap gracefully through the rough water.

Most of the afternoon we were in the rapids often with the boats half full of water but we were happy — happy as only those who love the wilds know how to be. The next day we reached Park Falls.

Dad joined us there and we continued the cruise. At Nine Mile Creek we stopped to fish for trout. After setting up camp each sought a place to try his luck. The brook was easily accessible nearby, but I wandered out across a boggy place to where the trees and brush grew dense along the brook's course. Much scrambling over logs and through brush soon brought me near the stream which rushed by silently and deep.

An ideal place for trout! The brook not ten feet across rushed swiftly out from a tunnel in the bushes above, slipped noiselessly between a grassy strip and the dense overhanging bushes opposite, then disappeared around a bend. All about me was the forest — not majestic — but still dark and lonesome, for the sky was leaden with threatening rain. Carefully I dropped my lure on the black waters just where they slipped out from the dense wall of bushes and let it float down to the bend, then, just as I was going to try again I felt that delightful little tug and a few minutes later part of our breakfast lay on the grass beside me in all its beauty.

II

The early hours of darkness were usually spent around the campfire, but there was one exception to that rule. We were comfortably fixed for a few days in a hunter's cabin — two of the party were trying a nearby trout stream while Scotty and I were getting supper, when the owner came along.

"Guess you boys'll have to move out," he said. "Some friends of mine are coming here tonight for a couple weeks' stay. There's another cabin about a mile down river that you can use, though."

The others soon came in and we packed up. We loaded my *Laura L* with all she would carry and after getting directions on how to find the other cabin, I pushed out leaving Dad and the others to gather up the rest of the duffel and follow in the *Pardner*.

It was already late dusk and the shore shadows on the river were creeping out into the current. The shores were high and dark and mysterious and awed me as I slipped along with the current. "Going pretty fast!" I thought. "Better watch closely for that clearing!" I

181

repeated my directions — "Go through two riffles, make a sharp bend to the right and on the third riffle is the cabin." I soon passed what I thought were the two riffles.

By now it was pitch dark and I was traveling by "feel." Then came the sharp turn, there was no mistaking it. "Must be pretty close," I thought and strained all my senses to locate a break in the shore line or catch the sound of rapids. On and on I paddled — "Surely I must have passed the place! I've gone over two miles, let alone one — wonder if that's it?" and I slid into the blackness of the shore, the boat grounded, but was swung off immediately by the current.

"Better take care; you're in the rapids, boy," and I tried it again with better luck. I got out and looked about, but no cabin. Once more I took up the paddle, thoroughly convinced I had travelled closer to three miles than one, but equally certain I had passed no cabin.

"Would the other boat ever catch up?" I grew more and more nervous for fear I had gone too far when the boat grounded sharply and swung off. I began to paddle hard to make a landing, for the current was fairly racing along. Again I struck bottom, though surely I was in mid stream. There was a snort and a splashing — then quiet. I had startled some night prowler.

No mention had been made of an island in my directions, but I was either on an island or a bar so I pushed out into the current. Quick as a flash I felt the boat jump ahead and the roar of rapids sounded clear and loud out of the stillness. Faster and faster I went, unable to see anything and hearing only the roar of the rapids. Surely it was a bad piece ahead; I couldn't tackle anything as bad as that at night, but the shore looked perpendicular and overhung with trees. What could I do?

Then, smash — bang! I stopped. A terrible snorting and thrashing in the water close by! a crashing of brush and limbs and several startling whistles, gradually getting farther away, a few sharp splashes at regular intervals farther down and then the crashing and whistling diminished to silence. How my heart pounded! No need to be afraid, to be sure, but the crashing of the deer as it bounded from the shallow water to the island then over to the mainland left me all atremble.

That settled it. I had not been told of any island and here most certainly was one. The water was so swift I could hardly hold a paddle in it. I concluded I had gone too far and set out to buck the current. I struggled and fought but seemed to make no headway, yet I dared not give up. After what seemed an age I heard the others call.

"You've passed it way back there."

It was the hardest paddle I ever made but at last we reached the clearing I had examined earlier. There was no cabin! It was then eleven o'clock so we pitched camp and turned in.

182

When we rolled out in the cold dawn we found ourselves in a burned over clearing scarce a quarter of a mile from the cabin we had left — yet at night we were all certain we had gone over a mile. Just below the island on the upper end of which I had grounded we found the cabin we had been looking for where we spent a couple of days.

III

After we left the cabin we found the rapids interesting. Below one pitch of Porcupine Rapids the *Pardner* landed a seven pound musky and we got a small bass. We safely navigated the first pitches of Wannigan Rapids and came on the third pitch on Flambeau Falls. It looked easy and the *Laura L* went ahead.

Next we knew we came smash upon a rather high ledge, scraped going over, and were plunged into seething, boiling water. The river suddenly narrows in a bend and all the water rushes at a large rock in mid stream. I saw the rock and saw the direction of the current, but try as I would there was no missing it entirely.

We struck broadside and it looked as if we would slide by with the water, but a submerged flat rock a little below the main obstruction held the bow fast so that the current forced the boat over and began to fill it. By crawling out on the high side we avoided more than a good wetting.

Before we could get free the *Pardner* came leaping along. Her crew saw the set of the current and worked like beavers to overcome its force, but in spite of all they could do the water dragged them as it had us. Fortunately for them we had usurped all grounding space. They just crashed into us and slid free. We bailed out, shot the rest of the swift water, and came out into the dead water near the South Fork.

At Cedar Rapids I missed the channel and struck a rock on the brink of the first drop. Dad managed to crawl out on the rock before the current caught the stem and plunged the boat into the rapids. I hung on and was dragged through the whole stretch — the saddest canoeist in the country. As soon as I could get the duffel laid out to dry I started back to get Dad. Before I got there, however, I saw his head bobbing along toward me. He had tried to wade ashore but slippery rocks and fast water soon had him swimming for his life.

I think the ducking did him good, for from then on his enjoyment of the trip increased and when he tells the story of that vacation somehow it always seems to begin, "When I swam the rapids —."

That afternoon we reached Beaver Dam Rapids. All possible channels looked wicked, so wicked in fact that we decided to portage

183

the duffel. When everything was ready and the cameras focused on the critical point the *Pardner* pushed out and aimed for the center of the channel.

As is often the case with rapids, once you have chosen your route the water carries you through with very little guiding on your part. Here it was a pretty ride all too quickly over. You quietly paddle out from shore and head your boat for that broad smooth lull of water. Slowly you draw nearer, then the force of the current catches you; you shoot forward, rise gracefully on the crest of the big wave and come down with a swish to rise again on the next and the next, and then cut into shore. Short as it is, that ride gives you joy for hours and makes the thought of portages lose its sting.

IV

We came upon Big Falls rather unexpectedly and found ourselves in the upper reaches of the rapids before we knew it. We had a bad time making shore and a hard tow to get back to the portage, but when we looked over that mile of heaving, tossing waves and cross currents and learned that one canoe lay in two parts on shore for trying to shoot through we set to with a will and made portage in a pouring rain.

The thing I remember about Big Falls, though, isn't the terrors of the river or the agonies of that mile and a quarter portage — it's the feed we got at the end. Mr. and Mrs. Collins of Chicago had a cabin at the end of the trail and when they saw us come down with the loads they asked us if we didn't want a cup of coffee. It proved to be a regular banquet.

It was about noon the next day when we landed above Little Falls. We looked it over from several points and had some argument about whether we should shoot or not.

"Well, let's portage the duffel anyway," Scotty said.

There is only one printable thing to be said about that portage — it does end and that not far from where it begins.

"That settles me!" I said as I dropped my load. "I don't carry a boat over that portage if there's water enough to float her around." The others agreed that a ducking was better than the portage.

"You going, Dad?" I asked when the *Pardner* was in quiet water.

"No, I hoodoed you on two rapids that were a lot tamer looking than these, and you got through Beaver Dam better alone than you would with me. Go ahead now."

I took up the paddle, got set, and glided out of the cove. Gee, it was a nasty looking mess to head into. It gave me a funny feeling in the pit of my stomach and yet there was that swift water fascination

184

that wouldn't let me turn back. Out around the point I paddled with long, heavy strokes, cut into the current, and shot ahead.

I wish I could describe the thrill that goes through you as you feel the force of the rapids on your craft and you race through the foam of the upper reaches. Faster and faster you go, paddling hard to have steerage way, watching the water ahead for rocks and the biggest waves which indicate deep water.

Then you hit the falls; the bow drops away suddenly and you shoot over. No sooner are you over than the bow leaps straight up on the first wave, part of which pours into the canoe from the sides if it happens to break at that moment. Down to level heel with a splash and up on the next wave you leap for all the world like a frightened animal, then you bound lightly over a few smaller waves and find yourself close to the treacherous back current.

If you have shipped much water as I did you may have trouble keeping clear and find your canoe headed for the falls again, but if you catch it in time, a few sharp back strokes will land you stem first by your duffel and you'll jump ashore to help get dinner.

V

From Ladysmith to the Chippewa River we found very quiet water, civilized scenery, and lots of clams. The Chippewa wasn't a great deal different and we soon reached Jim Falls dam.

We portaged the dam and were going to shoot the rapids below. A young chap who claimed to know the channels advised us to shoot on the left bank. None of the rapids on the Flambeau gave the trouble we met in trying to cross the Chippewa. Everything went wrong and we finally went over. The water was shallow, though, so that we could wade ashore. As there was no possible channel on that side and no portage, we worked back across the river.

After a careful scouting tour we shouldered our packs and scrambled over the rocks. The *Pardner's* crew decided to shoot with part of their load. We set the camera for a good picture.

All went well for the first two drops, except that the boat didn't rise much at the bottom. When they hit the main pitch the bow went clear out of sight. The water seemed all air and refused to float a boat. They made shore without tipping, thanks to the generous proportions of their boat, but the bow was badly stove where she hit a rock on the plunge.

"You can surely make it without any duffel," was their comment and I was quite as confident. It all went fine until I struck the big drop. I plunged just as they had done, in spite of the fact that on level heel

185

Laura's bow was way out of water. She righted, though, and I thought it was going to be a safe trip.

What happened next I can't tell and neither can the others who saw it, but in a flash I was swimming in the rapids.

I caught the long tow rope and tried to head shoreward. Two or three times I reached for the bottom, but there was no bottom, so I had to keep swimming. Slowly I edged out of the main current and it began to look as if I'd get ashore when the rope got tangled in my feet. I couldn't swim with my feet tied so I reached down and freed them but lost the rope in doing it. The current caught *Laura* again and whisked her out beyond reach. I kept on to shore.

By that time Scotty had launched the *Pardner* and started after the truant. To avoid going over the next falls he had to turn back without her. I quickly stripped and was put out on the rocks.

Two or three rods below was my overturned canoe but the water was fifteen or twenty feet deep and going like a mill race. It was many minutes before I got up courage enough to trust myself to the unknown powers and tricks of those undertows and cross currents, but at last I did.

I had hardly left the rock when I was crashed against the boat. I hung on and felt for the rock that was holding her but to my dismay I found the long rope had caught on some rocks fifty or sixty feet above. While I was resting on the canoe and wondering what to do next, the force of the current playing on my added weight snapped the rope and I found I was headed for another falls.

Catching hold of the broken rope I tried to tow the boat ashore but could not make any headway. I tried the nearest rocks with no better luck. I could not even hold my own against the current. I tried to swim it without the boat, but I might as well have tried to swim straight across Niagara for all the good it did. In spite of all I could do I was being steadily borne on to the falls and after a few quick thoughts I gave up the struggle and let the current carry me feet first.

Over the falls I went; down, down, down; would I never stop? Without waiting for an answer I struck out swimming under water in what I hoped was the direction of the shore. There seemed to be no rocks but plenty of deep water. I was so thoroughly scared that my strokes soon brought me out of it and I got to shore as quickly as I could.

Laura L went over the falls broadside. The current carried her on down and smashed her up on the rocks below.

■■■

About the Authors

We invited each author to send us some interesting information about his or her life. Here are their responses.

Jo and Jim Alderson are a husband-and-wife team. Says Jo Bartels Alderson, "I decided to be a writer at the age of eight and have never regretted the decision." She has had a book of poetry, *Owls,* published, and she and Jim wrote *The Man Mazzuchelli,* a biography of Wisconsin's pioneer priest. The Aldersons have coauthored numerous other works. Jim also confides, "I am heavily involved in the technical side of dramatics and am planning a book in the near future." The Aldersons live in Oshkosh.

Wanda Aukofer is a Milwaukee housewife and mother of seven children. She also worked at her husband's small print shop and continued the business many years after his death. "I started writing at 66 years of age," she says, "and have had about ten stories published."

Melba Baehr of Eau Claire enjoys reading and writing. Another hobby is rock hunting, which fascinates her because, she explains, "It takes me to all parts of the country and contains an element of mystery — in the thought that the piece of agate, fossil shell, or bit of coral I hold in my hand has lain hidden through the centuries, never seen or touched by another, until I came along and picked it up."

Ann Honeyager Baumgard, a graduate of Carroll College, taught for forty years in grade and high schools. Her first published book, *That's How It Was,* contained childhood memories of her life on a farm. Presently retired, she is actively involved in volunteer work and does much freelance writing. "Retirement is for the birds!" she says, "There are not enough days in a week!"

LaVerne H. Benson says, "I was born and raised in Kenosha. Father was a motorman in the city's streetcar system, and sometimes, when we brought him his lunch, he'd let us stand in front of him at the controls, and how we would clang the bell!"

Muriel J. Berger and her husband, David, now live in Florida, but Port Edwards was her home for many years. She taught in several central Wisconsin schools and will now teach at the Indian River Community College. "I listened to my father's stories of pioneer farm life," she recalls. "And from my grandfather, a foreman in the lumber camps, came the story about Frenchie's ghost."

Gerald Carlstein was born in West Allis in 1932. He has a degree in journalism from Marquette University and spent three years as a commissioned officer in the United States Navy. He is currently president of Fleet Services, Incorporated, of Milwaukee, a vehicle-leasing and fleet-management company.

Charles F. Church tells us he "lives with his wife, daughter, and three springer spaniels on a country lane south of Montello."

Louise Coleman graduated from the Boston Museum of Fine Arts School in sculpture and from Tufts University. After her marriage, she and her husband moved to Maryland. "Our trek with our two children from the Baltimore heat to the cool piney woods of Oneida County was a June occurrence for sixteen years." The Colemans now live in Madison. Louise adds, "I work as a freelance artist and help out at the State Historical Society as a docent and cataloguer."

Lester P. Coonen of Fort Atkinson was born and raised in Dundas, Calumet County, of a twelve-child family that operated a country store. He is a graduate of St. Norbert College and the University of Wisconsin and taught at De Sales College in Toledo and the University of Detroit. He is the author of eleven books and numerous articles on science and has done a few tongue-in-cheek newspaper stories. Coonen confides he has "an innate desire to string words together in phrases and sentences, then juxtapose and revise endlessly. Being married to a poet enhances this pleasurable misery."

William E. Daley of Milwaukee says, "My lifelong writing hobby took wings in early 1976 after open-heart surgery sent me into early retirement. My first sale, to *The Milwaukee Journal,* recounted a grandfather's baby-sitting adventures." Prior to his retirement, Daley worked as a reporter, a city editor, and for PPG Industries.

Mel Ellis is the well-known and widely read author of over a dozen books, including *Wild Goose, Brother Goose* and *This Mysterious River.* His many articles, in *The Milwaukee Journal,* particularly, and his syndicated column "The Good Earth" are read and remembered by

189

outdoors lovers everywhere. Ellis lives in Big Bend, where he has transformed fifteen acres of burned-out pastureland into a natural paradise with thousands of trees, hundreds of wildflowers, and four spring-fed ponds.

Gladys Reindahl Elviken was born in 1898, the daughter of Knute Reindahl, a world-renowned violin maker from Norway. After her graduation from St. Olaf College, she taught at the State School for Delinquent Girls in North Dakota. She and her husband, Andreas, moved abroad to study; he at Berlin University, she at the American Hospital in Paris. After her husband's death, in 1950, she continued to teach, this time delinquent girls in Connecticut. She now lives in Madison with her sister Olive, in the house built by their father.

Arline Ensenbach was born in Milwaukee and grew up in West Bend. She says, "I am married and have four children. I worked in sales and advertising before marriage. After the children were in school, I went back to work. I retired nine years ago." Her interests include crafts, travel, bowling, and, of course, writing."

Norma E. Erickson says, "I'm interested in historical research and reminiscence, and am busy organizing my notes on one of Wisconsin's famous women. I and my husband, John, celebrated our golden anniversary in 1981. We live in Edgerton with a black poodle named JAE."

Marie Felzo is a Milwaukee native, now living in Sheboygan. She studied in France under a Fulbright scholarship and was a teacher and play director in Michigan and Wisconsin high schools. Her previous writing includes a short story published in *Esquire*.

Edith Fleming has lived in the Town of Lake area since 1917. She writes that she and her husband, Gordon, "live on the edge of the forest with wildlife at our doorstep. My primary interests are the rural area and the recording of old logging sites and logging towns, where I grew up, married, and live."

Anastasia Furman of Oshkosh whimsically reveals, "I live in a farmhouse surrounded by trees and a garden where herbs, vegetables, and flowers naturalize with weeds. My cooking relies on basic ingredients, including whole-wheat flour and buckwheat (when I can find it). I don't touch bread when there's a boiled-in-the-jacket potato to eat with butter and onions sliced thin."

Michael Goc is a journalist and author who "shares a plot of Adams County marshland with my wife, Barbara Weade, our children, Nathan and Rachel, a thousand jack pines, and a pair of nesting sandhill cranes." Goc has written two books of local history and many stories about past and present country life in Wisconsin.

Laura M. Hansen was born near Glen Haven in 1894 and lived in Cassville. She was City Nurse in Rhinelander prior to her marriage. She began and wrote most of her autobiography during a five-year fight against a terminal illness. During her last stay in the hospital, she said, "I still have much more to write." She died in 1977.

Eleva D. Heimbruch of Royalton is a seventy-seven-year-old great-grandmother and an incurable optimist. She "likes music, poetry, creative writing, tiger kittens, beautiful sunsets, and children, but not in that order."

Jessie Eastman Holt tells us she was "born in Bear Creek and married John Reukauf, Jr., who was homesteading in Montana. We had two sons, Donald and William. In 1945 I joined Donald, who was working in Alaska. I had many exciting adventures there, including the adoption of a four-year-old native boy. My three sons live in Illinois, and I live in Prairie du Chien."

Margaret H. Holzman was born in Neenah in 1902. After graduating from Carroll College, she taught at Spring Valley, Kimberly, and Neenah high schools. At the age of fifty-three, she received her master's degree from Butler University, Indianapolis. She died in January of 1979.

Justin Isherwood is "a farmer of inexact methods in the practice of furrows, tending to potatoes, corn, maple syrup, and marsh hay. Father of two bairns; husband in as erotic a fashion as legal in broad day."

Catherine Whittier Lewis says, "In 1965 I organized the Fond du Lac Writers Workshop. I thought it would cause me to stop talking about writing and write. It did. Writing has been my joy, my frustration, my fun, my solace, my delight, my therapy, and always my shadow. I could do without many things, but not without my alter ego, my writing self."

Blanche B. Lindblad has won several awards, including one for an essay about a retarded child's private thoughts. "I've always liked to write," she confides, "and think best (even at age 76!) with a pencil in my hand. As a child, I read constantly and was curious about people and things. As for now, the writing bug still gives an occasional bite!''

Barbara Monteith Lunenschloss was born and reared in Montfort. She graduated from Platteville State Teachers' College and taught English in Belleville, New Glarus, and Spring Green. She and her husband, Neil, now reside in Spring Green.

Gertrude McGaffin was born in Milwaukee and had her first experience in carnival life while in high school. ''I joined the carnival and followed the circuit for the next seven years. Worked illusions, sold tickets, and eventually learned to swallow a neon sword.'' From the carnival, she moved into farming, ''which held many challenges for someone who had never been to a farm.''

Linda Myer now lives in Cambridge, Massachusetts. Last year she coauthored and published a book on public interest group lobbying. She works as a freelance editor, writes and performs poetry, and acts in local theater groups. This year she plans to write a theater piece based on women's history.

Alonzo W. Pond is a traveler, scientist, writer, archeologist, and anthropologist. From 1906 to 1980, he has published fifteen books and hundreds of articles. His exploits include driving an ambulance in World War I and exploring the Sahara, Gobi, and Arabian deserts. At 89, he lives in Minocqua with his wife, Dorothy.

Sara Rath has written many articles and screenplays and is the author of five published books. Her latest book, *Remembering the Wilderness,* contains poems from the past ten years, ''a time of transition from wife and mother to a more independent person.'' Her work has won awards from the Council for Wisconsin Writers and the Chicago International Film Festival, among others. Now living in Middleton, she writes and produces for public television in Madison.

Gladys M. Rebelein of Platteville writes, ''My childhood was spent on a farm. During the Depression I taught at a rural school for $45 a month. I married a pastor; we have four children. After they were grown, I taught junior high English. I enjoy writing real-life stories because it enables me to relive the past and share it with others.''

George A. Richard, Jr. is an Illinois native, but says, ''Wisconsin (and in particular Kewaunee County) has always been my first love. My roots go back to the days of the earliest settlers. Thanks to my maternal grandparents, I developed a sense and appreciation of this area's background, which I hope to pass on to the next generation.''

Jack Rudolph writes, ''Retired Regular Army colonel (West Point Class of 1933) and newspaperman, now a freelance writer. Specialty is history, both national and regional.'' Among his awards is one from the National Writers Club. Rudolph has written for *Sports Illustrated, American Heritage,* and many other magazines.

Dorothy B. Schmitz of Middleton came from Indiana University with a theater background. She was also the moving force behind the University of Wisconsin's Adult Education Center. It was through her efforts that older adults were invited to audit classes. At age seventy-five, she ran for a council seat in Middleton (winning by a clear mandate of fifteen votes). Now eighty-two, she feels strongly that the elderly are still vital, active people and should be recognized as such by the community. ''Just don't give up,'' she says.

Clay Schoenfeld is a professor of journalism and mass communication and holds several other posts in conservation and education at the University of Wisconsin-Madison. He has written numerous articles and is the author of twenty-five books, including *Down Wisconsin Sideroads.*

Margaret I. Shale of North Freedom taught rural school before her marriage. She and her husband ran a dairy farm and raised four children. She began writing, after the age of fifty, by creating travelogues of the cross-country trips she and her husband took. At eighty-eight, she still keeps active with her writing and is well-known in her area as a writer, poet, and church historian.

Buz Swerkstrom is a freelance writer who holds up his end of the world in Atlas, Wisconsin. His publication credits include *Ford Times, The Milwaukee Journal, True West,* and *Wisconsin trails.*

Samuel H. Thut of Madison says it was his ''rural woodland origin and experiences that led to a lifetime interest in logging and construction.'' As a boy, he helped his family develop a farm from forest land; as an adult, he worked every job in commercial logging, from ''swamper'' to ''camp boss.'' Now eighty-two, he still cuts and splits his own firewood.

■■■